BIBLE BLESSINGS.

THE HEATHEN FATHER.

Bible Blessings. FRONTISPIECE. p. 25.

BIBLE BLESSINGS.

BY THE

REV. RICHARD NEWTON, D.D.,

AUTHOR OF "RILLS FROM THE FOUNTAIN OF LIFE," "THE BEST THINGS," "KING'S HIGHWAY," "GIANTS, AND HOW TO [illegible]HEM," "THE SAFE COMPASS," ETC.

NEW YORK:

ROBERT CARTER & BROTHERS,

No. 530 BBOADWAY.

1868.

J. H TOBITT,
Printer and Stereotyper,
Franklin-square.

E. O. JENKINS,
Printer,
20 *North William-st.*

CONTENTS.

PREFACE.

WHEN the children of Israel had reached the borders of the land of Canaan, Moses sent some men to go up and see what kind of a land it was, and to bring back some specimens of its fruit. Among other things which those men brought, were some bunches of grapes, so large and fine that they had to be carried on a pole borne on the shoulders of two of their number. What noble samples those were of the rich fruit that grew in "that good land," which God had promised to give to the children of Israel!

In preparing this little volume I feel as if I had been doing very much the same thing that was done by those spies. I have been walking, as it were, through the pleasant fields of the Bible, and gathering specimens of its blessings. The Bible is a book of blessings. It is intended to make people happy in this life, as well as in the life to come. It would take, not one book merely, but a whole library of books, to tell of all the blessings spoken of in the Bible. If the few samples of them here presented shall lead any one who reads this book to love the Bible more, and to seek a larger share in the rich store of its blessings, I shall feel abundantly rewarded for the labor bestowed upon it.

R. N.

I.

The Blessedness of Hearing the Gospel.
The Evils from which it Saves Us.

"Blessed are the people that know the joyful sound."
PSALM lxxxix. 15.

I.

"Blessed are the people that know the joyful sound."
PSALM lxxxix. 15.

WHAT a pleasant thing it is to go through a garden, full of flowers! As you walk quietly along, you can pluck one flower here and another there, till you have gathered a beautiful boquet. And then how pleasant it is to stop and look at them, and admire the beauty of their form and color, and enjoy the sweet fragrance which they yield!

We may compare the Bible to such a garden. Each chapter in this blessed book is like a bed in the garden. The precious promises of the Bible are like the flowers which bloom, and the fruits which ripen in this garden. These flowers and fruits are very numerous, and very different from each other, but all very beautiful. When we are reading and studying the Bible, we are, as it were, walking up and down in God's flower-garden. And when we stop to examine one verse after another, we are plucking the flowers and gathering the fruit that grow there. And in beginning another course of sermons for our Children's Church, I feel as if you and I were just starting off, on a fresh walk, through the beautiful spiritual garden which God has planted for us in his wonderful book. We are going to talk about "*Bible Blessings.*" I mean by this the blessings which the Bible brings to us. And while we are doing this, it seems to me as if we shall just be walking about in God's garden, and gathering a boquet of the beautiful flowers which are growing there. I hope we may all find a great deal of pleasure and profit from this course of sermons, or from this ramble through God's beautiful garden.

Our first sermon will be on the words—"Blessed are the people that know the joyful sound."

Here the Bible is spoken of as if it were a trumpet, and those who hear this trumpet are said to be blessed. Let us see, before going any further, if we understand what this means.

Now you know that the Jews used to have what they called "the year of Jubilee." This came once in every fifty years. Suppose that a Jew, in old times, had become so poor that he had to sell his home, his house and lands; or suppose he had even to sell himself, as a servant or slave, which they did sometimes. Well, when the year of Jubilee came, the man who had sold his house would get it back again, without paying any thing for it. And the man who had sold himself into bondage, would cease to be a slave. He would get his liberty again for nothing. And as soon as the first day of the year of Jubilee came in, trumpets were blown all through the land. When the sound of those trumpets was heard the people knew that the year of Jubilee was come. Then all the people who had been obliged to sell their homes went back to them again, and all those who had been sold as slaves became free.

We can easily understand, therefore, what a joyful thing the sound of that trumpet must have been to many among the Jews, and how blessed those were who heard it.

Now heaven is our Father's house, which we have lost by sin. And sin has not only lost us that house, but has sold us to Satan, as his slaves. But the Bible brings to us a year of Jubilee. It comes to tell us how we may escape from being the slaves of Satan, and get back to heaven, our Father's house again. This is the meaning of that beautiful Sunday School hymn;—

Blow ye the trumpet, blow
 The gladly solemn sound!
Let all the nations know,
 To earth's remotest bound,
The year of Jubilee has come;
Return, ye ransom'd sinners, home.

Ye who have sold for naught,
 The heritage above,
Can have it back, unbought,
 The gift of Jesu's love.

The gospel trumpet hear,
  The news of pardoning grace;
Ye happy souls, draw near,
  Behold your Saviour's face;
The year of Jubilee is come;
Return, ye ransom'd sinners, home.

We begin our course of sermons on "Bible Blessings" by speaking of *the blessedness of having the Bible.* This is what our sermon is about to-day—*The blessedness of having the Bible.* It is a blessed thing to have the Bible *because of the evils from which it saves us.* If we live till next month, we must have another sermon on this subject to show that it is a blessed thing to have the Bible *because of the benefits it brings us.*

"Blessed are the people that know the joyful sound."

It is a blessed thing to have the Bible *because of the evils from which it saves us.*

I wish to speak of *four* different kinds of evils from which the Bible saves us. And we shall see that each of these evils furnishes us with a good reason why it may be said,

"Blessed are the people that know the joyful sound."

The first evil from which the Bible saves us is IGNORANCE.

Ignorance is to our minds just like what darkness is to our bodies. It prevents us from seeing the things around us. When the sun is shining brightly, how pleasant it is to look out on a beautiful landscape! We can see the green fields and the waving grain,—the trees, the hills, the streams, and every thing. But suppose the sun should suddenly be taken away. Could we see any thing then? No. All would be dark around us. We could see nothing. Now the Bible is like a sun to us. It sheds light on a great many things. If it were not for the Bible, we should be left in the dark on all these things. The Bible drives away this darkness. It saves us from ignorance. But we are so accustomed to the Bible, and the blessed light which shines from it, that we hardly know how to prize it enough, or what our condition would be if we had never had it. If we want to know what a blessed thing it is to hear its joyful sound, we must look at the ignorance of some of the people who have never had the Bible.

Sometimes when the missionaries of the gospel go to the heathen, to teach them about Jesus and his religion, they have to begin first to teach them the English language, because many of the languages of the heathen have no words to express some of the most important things of which the missionaries wish to speak. Some of those languages have no word to stand for the "*soul*," or "life," or "home," or "mercy," or "heaven," or "eternity." Now suppose we lived among a people who knew nothing about "home—sweet home." That is, suppose none of us had any home. Suppose that we did not know that there was such a thing as *mercy*—or such a place as heaven? Suppose that we did not know that we had a *soul*—and that we are to live after death—how sad our state would be! That would be like being in the dark indeed! How dreadful such ignorance would be! And yet if it were not for the Bible we should be ignorant about these things, or left in the dark about them.

But there are a great many other things of which people are left in ignorance, who are without the Bible.

The people who live in Hindostan, you know, are called Hindoos. They pride themselves on their learning. They have no Bible like ours. But they have a great many sacred books which are called Shasters, or Vedas. These books profess to teach the Hindoos what they must believe, not only about religion, but about history, and botany, and natural philosophy, and astronomy, and geography. But a great many of the things contained in the Vedas are so foolish, that the people had better, a great deal, be left without any teaching at all, than be taught anything so silly and ridiculous.

For instance, let us just see what the Vedas, or sacred books of the Hindoos, teach them on the subject of geography. Now if I

MOUNT MERU
160000 MILES
840000 MILES
50000 MILES

HINDOO MAP OF THE WORLD.

should ask you some questions in geography, like these: What is the shape of the earth? how many miles is it in circumference? how many in diameter? what proportion of the earth is land? and what is water? what are the four continents of the earth called? and what are the names of the principal rivers and mountains? some of the children even in the Infant School could answer them. And the children who could give these answers are much wiser, on this subject, than the men who wrote those sacred books of the Hindoos, or than the Brahmins, or priests are who teach them to the people.

On the opposite page is a representation of the Hindoo map of the world, or the system of geography which they are taught. It is very curious. On this map, or picture, are two circles. The one on the left represents the world as inhabited by men and animals. You see, on it, six long ranges of mountains, running, as we should say, from north to south, and two shorter ones, running across them from east to west. In the centre of this circle is a wonderful mountain called Meru. This mountain, the Hindoos say, is made up of gold and jewels, and is the place where their gods dwell. Meru is said to be eight hundred and forty thousand miles high. And what is more remarkable still, is, that unlike all other mountains, which get smaller as they rise higher, this mountain is as wide again at the top as it is at the bottom. The base is said to be eighty thousand miles wide, while the summit is a hundred and sixty thousand. This Mount Meru is supposed to be the centre of the earth. At the base of it are four other mountains which support it. From these mountains flow out four rivers, represented by the waved lines on the map. And on each of these mountains is an enormous tree, eight thousand eight hundred miles high! This plain which lies around the foot of Mount Meru is said to be four thousand millions of miles in width!

Outside of this plain is a set of seven seas, or oceans, which surround the earth like so many vast rings, or circles. These are represented in the figure on the right hand of the map. The first of these seas is of salt water. Then follows a belt of earth; then the second sea, which is of the juice of the sugar-cane; then another belt of earth, and the third sea, which is of wine, and so on. The fourth sea is of melted butter, the fifth of sweet milk, the sixth of curdled milk, and the seventh of fresh water.

Now what a system of geography this is! And things just as foolish are taught in those books about the sun, and the moon, and the stars, and many other things. And yet the Hindoos are considered one of the most intelligent heathen nations in the world.

But if it was only about geography and astronomy, and such like subjects, that we should be left in ignorance, without the Bible, it would not be of so much consequence. But this is not all. Without the Bible, we never could tell certainly whether we have souls or not. If we knew that we had, we never could tell what was to become of them when we die. We could not tell whether there is a heaven or not; and if there is, how we are to get there. We could not tell how the world was made, or what is to become of it hereafter. There would be no sun to shine upon our souls. We should be left like people who are groping their way in the dark. There would be nothing for us to do but to go stumbling on, all our days,—and at last to make a dreadful plunge in the dark, without knowing, at all, where that plunge would take us.

But—" Blessed are the people that know the joyful sound." It is a blessed thing to have the Bible, because of the evils from which it saves us. The *first of these evils is ignorance.*

The second of these evils is OPPRESSION.

I suppose you all know what oppression means. For instance. Here is a little boy going out into the fields to fly a kite which he has just made. A big boy meets him, and threatens to beat him, unless he gives him the kite. There is no one near to help the little boy. He is obliged to give up his kite, and let the big boy take it. That would be oppression. You might well say that that big boy was oppressing the little boy. And wherever anything like this is done, by one man towards another, *that* is oppression.

In this country we have laws to protect those who are poor and weak, so that those who are richer and stronger than they, cannot injure or oppress them. I may be one of the poorest men in this city; yet no man, however rich or great he is, has any right to come into my house, and take away anything that belongs to me, without my consent. If any one should attempt to do this, the law would protect me. I could have the man taken up and put in prison.

But in many heathen countries, where they have never had the Bible, they have no laws to protect the people. The chiefs, and great men, can oppress the poor people, and take away their property, and even their lives, and there is nothing to stop them. In New Zealand, and in the Fiji Islands, the chief of a tribe, or district, could enter the dwellings of the people, and if he saw any thing that he wanted, no matter how much the owner valued it, he would quietly take it himself, or send one of his servants to take it, and no one durst say a word.

Now it is very sad to think of wicked men having such power over the *property* of others; but it is still more dreadful to think of their having the same power over *the lives* of others. Yet this is the case in many heathen countries. In China a father can do what he likes with the lives of his children, and there is no law to punish or prevent him. A missionary knew of a Chinese father who said to his wife—"What shall we do with our young son? He won't mind what we say. Let us put him to death." The mother consented. They tied a rope round the poor boy's neck. The father took hold of one end, and the mother the other, and they pulled away till they strangled the child. The dreadful deed was well known in the neighborhood, but no one took any notice of it.

There was a man living in the city of Ningpo, in China, who had two sons. One of them did something which displeased his father. He resolved to get rid of him. The next day he ordered his two sons to follow him to the river. Then they all got into a boat and rowed into the middle of the stream. Then the father tied a large stone round the son's neck, and made his brother assist, while he threw the wretched boy into the water, where he sank to rise no more. How sad to think of such things!

But though *boys* are sometimes treated in this way in China, the *girls* are served much worse. There is no telling what numbers of them are killed while they are infants. In the city of Amoy there is a large place, full of water, which is called "the Girl's Ditch." Into this as many as a dozen female infants are sometimes thrown alive at one time, and no one takes any more notice of them than if they were so many kittens, or mice.

One time, some years ago, an English merchant was lodging for a night in the house of a chief, on the island of New Zealand. A servant girl belonging to the chief came in. She had been away, somewhere, for two days. Without waiting to ask where she had been, or why she had been away, her mistress told one of the men standing by to kill her. With one blow of his axe he struck her dead. In the evening of the same day a large party of friends feasted on her body, and her head was given to the children for a plaything.

One day, several years ago, a chief in this same island ordered one of his female servants to heat a large oven, as he was going to have a feast for his friends in the evening. She did so. When the oven was made very hot, to her great horror, her master ordered her to throw herself into it. Poor creature! she begged—she cried for mercy, she threw herself on the ground, and clasped her cruel master's knees, and prayed him to pity, and spare her, but it was all of no use. He was not angry with her. She had not done any thing to displease him, only he wanted to have a feast of human flesh. So he seized the poor girl, tied her hands and feet, and flung her alive into the heated oven! And there was no law to punish that wicked man!

But they have the Bible in New Zealand now. The Bible has given them laws which stop this oppression. The people of New Zealand have heard the joyful sound of the gospel. They can understand, much better than we can, what a blessed thing it is to hear that sound. It is a blessed thing to hear this joyful sound, because of the evils from which it saves us.

The second of these evils is *oppression.*

The third evil from which the Bible saves us is—CRUELTY.

Wherever the Bible is not known, cruelty prevails, in many forms. We read in the Bible, that—"The dark places of the earth are *full* of the habitations of cruelty." Ps.

lxxiv. 20. These dark places mean heathen lands. Wherever you go in heathen lands, you meet with cruelty in one form or other. I know that this is not a pleasant subject to dwell upon. But we cannot tell how much we owe to the Bible, or what a blessed thing it is to hear this joyful sound, unless we do, in this way, look at the dreadful evils from which we are saved by having the Bible. And one of the worst of these evils is the cruelty which prevails in lands where the Bible is not known.

One of these forms of cruelty is *the offering of human sacrifices.*

Not long since there was war on the west coast of Africa. One of the tribes, before going to battle, resolved to offer a sacrifice to their god, in order to secure success. They selected a little boy, about eight years old, as their victim. They dressed him in the nicest clothes they had. They decorated his fingers and toes with gold rings, and hung around his neck greegrees, or charms. Then they placed him in a deep hole, with his head just above the ground. The poor little fellow cried, and screamed, but nobody minded him. A great crowd of men and women stood round, and watched what was done. They filled up the hole with earth and stones. They piled it up over his head till a great mound was raised above him, and then they left him, in his living grave, to die a miserable death. All through Africa such dreadful sacrifices are offered from time to time.

Another way in which the cruelty of heathen lands shows itself is in *the treatment of parents by their children.*

In the Fiji Islands, when the parents of a family get old, the children will tell them that "it's time for them to be going." Then they will give them the choice of the way in which they may prefer to die. The usual ways are either by strangling, or burying alive. When the choice is made, the family and friends come together to assist in getting them out of the way. And when it is all over, they have a feast together in honor of the occasion.

In India, instead of burying their parents alive, they carry them to the banks of the river Ganges, and leave them there to die.

Some time ago, the aged father of a Hindoo family was taken sick. His sons wanted to get him out of the way, that they might share his property between themselves. They carried him to the Ganges, and placing him with his feet in the water, they left him there to die, without any one to help or pity him. But instead of dying, he got better, and managed, after awhile, to get back to his home. Instead, however, of welcoming him back, and treating him kindly, his cruel sons ridiculed and cursed him; they abused him, and drove him away from his home. The poor old man, broken-hearted at the conduct of his unnatural sons, went sorrowing back to the river, and threw himself in, and was drowned.

And so we might go on to speak of cannibalism, or the eating of human flesh, and a great many other forms of cruelty which are found in heathen lands; but from all these evils we are delivered, because we are blessed in hearing the joyful sound of the gospel.

Cruelty is the third evil from which the Bible saves us.

The fourth and last evil of which I would speak, from which the Bible saves us, is— IDOLATRY.

I might speak of many things which show us how dreadful it is to be an idolator, but I will only speak of *two*. One of these is the *character of the idol gods*;—the other is the *kind of sacrifices offered to them.*

The heathen have a great multitude of gods. I will only take two, as specimens. The rest are all very much like them. The two, that I refer to, are the god Siva, and Kalee, his wife. Siva is one of the millions of false gods worshipped in India. In a picture, which I have of him, he is represented as having twenty-five heads, rising up one above the other, in the form of a pyramid, and thirty-two arms and hands. Each of these thirty-two hands holds some weapon for punishing, or destroying. In one there is a bow, in another an arrow, in another a sword—a knife—a knotted rope—a spear—a club—a sling—a red-hot iron, or some such deadly weapon. What a strange figure this is! I suppose the twenty-five heads are put upon this god to show how much knowledge he has, and the thirty-two arms and hands to show how much power he has. But then it seems that all this knowledge, and all this power, are only employed for the purpose of punishing, and destroying men. The heads are intended to guide the hands in using the weapons of destruction which they hold. There is nothing in such a god that people can love, but everything for them to fear. Among all his many heads and hands, not one of them is employed in helping or comforting those who worship him; they are all intended to alarm, and terrify, and punish.

And Kalee, the wife of Siva, is just what we might expect the wife of such a monster to be. She is represented as having four arms. In one is a sword—in another is the head of a giant, and so on. Around her neck she wears a long necklace of human skulls, while everything about her tells of cruelty and bloodshed.

What a dreadful thing it must be to have to worship such horrible beings as these! When we kneel down to worship our God and Saviour, we think how pure, how holy, how kind and good He is, and the very thought of Him helps to make us better. But to think of such a god as Siva or Kalee, would never make any body feel better, but only worse.

The character of these gods shows what a dreadful thing idolatry is. And then *the kind of sacrifices offered to them* shows the same thing.

Some years ago a missionary in India went with some friends to the temple of Siva, the god of whom we have just spoken, to see the people offering sacrifices. A great crowd of people were in the temple. One of the priests stood before the idol, with a sharp knife in his hand. He was helping the people to offer their sacrifices. And what were they? One man came up. The priest told him to open his mouth and put his tongue out. He did so. The priest seized hold of his tongue, and cut a slit in it with his knife. *That* was his offering. Another man came. The priest told him to uncover the side of his body. He did so. The priest pinched up the flesh with his thumb and finger, ran his knife through the flesh, and thrust a stick through the opening. That was his offering. And so they went on.

Some years ago, before the gospel had been introduced into the South Sea Islands, they were having service in an idol temple, on one of those islands. In the midst of the service, the priest stopped, and looked round upon the people. He wanted to get an offering that he thought his god would be particularly pleased with. He saw a man sitting not far from the idol. He stole up softly behind him. With one blow of his club he broke the man's neck, and then he instantly scooped out one of his eyes, put it on a green leaf, and presented that as an offering to his god. How dreadful!

Some time ago, a rich merchant in India had been unfortunate in business, and lost all his money. He thought his god was angry with him, and that he must offer some great sacrifice to secure his favor. He went to consult a priest. The priest told him that all persons who would offer themselves, and what they loved best, to their god, on a particular day, would be sure to please him. The poor ignorant man believed the wicked priest. He resolved to offer the greatest sacrifice in his power. When the day came, he heaped a great pile of wood in his house. He cut the throats of his three children, threw their bodies on the pile, and set it on fire. Then he plunged the knife into his own body, and flung himself upon the blazing pile.

Such are the sacrifices offered by the heathen to their gods. What a dreadful thing idolatry is, when we think of the character of the idol gods, and the kind of sacrifices offered to them.

"Blessed are the people that know the joyful sound" of the gospel. It is a blessed thing to hear this sound, because of the evils from which it saves us.

We have spoken of *four* of these evils The *first is ignorance—the second oppression —the third cruelty—and the fourth idolatry.*

How thankful we should be to Jesus for bringing his gospel to us! Blessed are our eyes for the things which they see, and our ears for the things which they hear. How many kings, and prophets, and righteous men, in old times, desired to see the things which we see, but "died without the sight!" If it were not for the blessed gospel of Jesus, *we* might, even now, be suffering from the ignorance, the oppression, the cruelty, and the idolatry of which we have been speaking. How much do we owe to Jesus for saving us from all these evils! Shall we not make Him an offering? But what is the most acceptable offering we can make? O nothing like those cruel, bloody ones which the heathen offer to their gods. No. Jesus says, "Give me thine *heart*." This is the best offering we can make. To love Him—to serve Him, and try to become like Him—this is the offering He desires. Let us all make this offering.

And then, there is one other thing we can do. We can try to send the gospel to others. Let us resolve to take a fresh interest in the missionary cause. Let us do more, and give more, and pray more for it. This will show that we understand the meaning, and feel the truth of the text, which says—"Blessed are the people that know the joyful sound."

II.

The Blessedness of Hearing the Gospel.
The Benefits it Brings.

"Blessed are the people that know the joyful sound."
PSALM lxxxix. 15.

II.

PSALM lxxxix. 15. "Blessed are the people that know the joyful sound."

IN talking about these words last month, I tried to show you that it is a blessed thing to hear the joyful sound of the gospel, because of the evils from which it saves us. I spoke of four kinds of evils from which the gospel saves us. These were *ignorance—oppression—cruelty*—and *idolatry*. I wish now to show that it is a blessed thing to hear the joyful sound of the gospel *because of the benefits which it brings to us.*

But who can tell all the benefits which the gospel brings to us? Suppose some one should set you down by the sea shore, and ask you to count all the grains of sand that are lying on there, could you do it? No. You might take up a handful of the sand and count a few hundreds, or thousands of grains but you would soon give it up, and find it impossible to count them all. And we shall find it very much the same when we try to count up all the blessings that we owe to Jesus, or all the benefits that His gospel brings to us. Some people think that all that Jesus does for His people is to pardon their sins, and take them to heaven when they die. But this is a mistake. It is true indeed that to get our sins pardoned is a very great blessing. And, to be sure of going to heaven, when we die, is *so great* a blessing, that if the *whole world* were ours, and we should give the world, with all that is in it, for this privilege, it would be a cheap price to pay for such a blessing. But these are not all the benefits that the gospel brings to us. Jesus has brought us blessings for our *bodies* as well as for our *souls*. He has brought blessings for us in *this* world, as well as in the world to come. The fact is, that *all* the blessings we have here, we owe to Jesus. It was said of Jesus before He was born, "that all the people in the world should be *blessed in*

Him." And this is true. When Adam and Eve sinned in the garden of Eden, if Jesus had not promised to die for their sins, they would have been destroyed, and then you and I never would have lived at all. So you see we owe our lives to Jesus. All the men, and women, and children in the world, yes, and all the animals too—the birds in the air, the beasts on the earth, and the fishes in the sea—owe their lives to Jesus. If Jesus had not promised to die for us, this great globe on which we live would have been destroyed. Jesus died to save the *world itself* from destruction, as well as the people that live in it. A great many people never think of this. But it is true. We owe the bright sunshine, that lights up the world, to Jesus. The trees and flowers that make the earth look so beautiful, we owe to Jesus. The air we breathe, the strength we feel, the health we enjoy, the food we eat, the water we drink, the clothes we wear, the homes in which we live, and the friends we love, and whose presence makes our homes so sweet and pleasant—*all these* we owe to Jesus. But some of these are benefits or blessings, which Jesus gives even to the heathen, who have never heard "the joyful sound" of the gospel.

There are other blessings, however, which Jesus brings only to those who do hear the sound of the gospel. These are "*The Bible Blessings*" of which I especially desire to speak. I might speak of a great many benefits or blessings which the gospel brings to us, but I will only mention *three.*

It is a blessed thing to hear the joyful sound of the gospel *because of the benefits which it brings to us.*

The first of these benefits of which I would speak is—KNOWLEDGE.

In our last sermon I said that the first of the evils from which the gospel saves us is *ignorance.* And now, in talking about the benefits which the gospel brings us, it is proper to begin by speaking of the wonderful knowledge which it gives us. Knowledge is like light. It helps us to see things clearly, and to understand all about them; but if we were left without knowledge, these things would seem to us just as if they were in the dark. For instance, here we are in this church. We have plenty of light here. You can see me, and I can see you. We can see the persons in the gallery. We can see the windows, and the doors. We can see the way in, and the way out. We can see every thing we want to see here plainly. But, suppose now all this light were taken away, and it should suddenly become dark, inky, pitchy, totally dark. We could not see one another then. But still we could *feel* our way into the aisle, and so on, towards the door, for we should know there were doors, and just where we should find them. But suppose we had never been in the church before; and suppose we were brought in here at midnight, and left here without a single ray of light. Then we should not know where the pulpit was, or the aisle, or the windows, or the doors. We should not know how we got into the church, or how it would be possible for us to get out.

We should have no knowledge of the church. We should be in the dark about it. And just so, if we had no Bible, we should have no knowledge of the things about which the Bible tells us. We should be in the dark about them. We should be in the dark about ourselves, where we came from, and where we are going to. We should be in the dark about the world we live in, about how it was made, and what it was made for. We should be in the dark about our own hearts, how sin got in there, and how we can get it out. We should be in the dark about God. We should not know whether He was like the gods that the heathen worship, or not. In regard to all these things, which it is of the utmost importance for us to know about, we should be entirely in the dark. We might go groping, and stumbling about, and trying to feel our way, but we never should succeed. Nobody could give us any light, or knowledge in regard to these things.

There are a great many things about which we can find out all the knowledge we want, without the Bible. If I want to get a knowledge of geography, for example, I need not go to the Bible for this. And so, if I want to get a knowledge of arithmetic, or history, or botany, there are other books besides the Bible, which will tell me all I wish to know, on these subjects. If a physician wants to get a knowledge of some particular kind of disease, and how it may be cured, he can find out all about it without going to the Bible. If a sailor wants to find out how to navigate a ship;—or a farmer how to plow his field, and cultivate his farm, he can get this kind of knowledge without the help of the Bible. If I want to learn how to build a house, or a ship, how to make a coat, or a pair of shoes, it is not necessary for me to go to the Bible for light, or knowledge on these subjects. The Bible was not intended to teach us anything about such matters. We can get all this kind of knowledge that we need without the Bible. But there are a great many other things which we should never have known at all, and about which nobody, in the world, could give us the least light, or knowledge, if it were not for the Bible. Suppose you want to know how to worship, and serve God ; if there were no Bible, who could tell you ? Suppose you feel the wickedness of your heart, and want to know how you can get it changed, so as to be made happy in this world; let the Bible be taken away, and who can tell you ? Suppose you want to know what is to become of you when you die, and how you can be sure of being happy forever; if we had no Bible, where could you get this knowledge ? You might read all the books in the world, and ask all the wisest men that ever lived, and you would not get the least knowledge on these important subjects. We should be in the dark about them. Nobody would be able to throw a ray of light upon them. But we open the Bible, and, like the sun in the heavens, it sheds at once, a flood of light upon them all. It tells us *how* the world was made, and what it was made for. It tells us how *sin got into* our hearts, and how we may *get it out* again.

It tells us what kind of a God Jesus our Saviour is, and how we may serve and please Him, and enjoy his favor here. It tells us what must become of us when we die, and points out to us the path in which we must walk if we wish to get to heaven at last, and be happy with God forever. And therefore we may well say—"Happy are the people that know the joyful sound." It is a blessed thing to hear the gospel, because of the benefits which it brings to us. The first of these benefits is *knowledge*.

The second benefit which the gospel brings to those who hear its joyful sound is—PARDON.

The greatest evil under which any body in the world ever suffered is sin. And the greatest blessing, or benefit any body can receive is to get rid of sin. But to get rid of sin is to have it pardoned. The *pardon* of sin is a blessing worth more than all the gold and silver in the world put together. But perhaps some of you may be ready to ask, well, if the pardon of sin is really such a very great blessing, why don't people try more to get it? This is a very proper question to ask just here. The answer to it is this: people do not value the pardon which Jesus brings, because they do not see and feel what a dreadful evil sin is. If they could only see this in its proper light, as God sees it, they would never rest, and never have any peace or comfort till they were sure of a pardon. When God speaks of sin, He calls it "the *abominable* thing that *He hates.*" Now there are two things that we must do if we wish to know what sort of an evil sin is, and how great a blessing the pardon is that Jesus gives to His people. One of these things is, *to look at what the Bible says about sin. The other is to see what dreadful things men are sometimes willing to suffer in the hope of getting their sins pardoned.*

Now let us see what the Bible says about sin. Let us look at one or two of the things to which it is compared in the Bible. *Sometimes the Bible compares sin to a burden.* David speaks of it in this way when he says,

Psalm xxxviii. 4, "Mine iniquities are as *a heavy burden*, too heavy for me." And Jesus Himself uses this comparison when He says, Matt. xi. 28, "Come unto me all ye that labor, and are *heavy laden*, and I will give you rest." Sin is a burden to the *soul*, not to the body. But we all know what it is for the body to have to carry a heavy burden. Suppose you had such a burden bound upon your shoulders. Suppose it was so heavy as to bow you down so that you could not stand upright. Suppose, too, that it was fastened to you in such a way that you never could take it off for a moment. You have to lie down with it at night when you go to bed. You get up with it in the morning when you rise. You have to carry it with you wherever you go. At home, in the street, in school, at church, wherever you are, you are obliged to go bending, and staggering, and groaning under this burden. How dreadful this would be! And if this were the case with you, what would be the *one thing*, which, above all others, you would consider a blessing, and desire to have? To get rid of this burden. That is true. And the pardon which Jesus gives is getting rid of the burden of sin. And when we feel sin to be a burden, the pardon of it will appear to us as the greatest blessing that we can receive.

But there is another view of sin in the Bible. *The sin which belongs to our fallen nature is compared to a dead body; and we are represented as chained to this dead body, and obliged to drag it about with us wherever we go.* This is what St. Paul means when he says—Rom. vii. 24—"O wretched man that I am, who shall deliver me from *the body of this death?*"—or, from *this dead body.* To chain a person to a dead body was one of the modes of punishment used by ancient tyrants. Only think of being chained to a dead body, a ghastly, putrefying corpse, and never being able to get away from it, for a moment! How horrible! Why, the very thought of it makes one's blood run cold. Now, if this were your condition, what would you consider the greatest blessing, or benefit that could possibly be conferred upon you? You would say, in a moment—"O take away this dreadful thing! Break the chain that binds me to it, and let me get away, where I shall never see it again." And suppose that some one should come and offer to give you the finest house in the country, or even to make you a king, and secure you a crown and a palace, would you be willing to accept the offer, if it was necessary that you should always remain chained to that dreadful corpse? Certainly not. But sin is just like such a dead, decaying body. We are bound, or chained to it. No one can break the chain which binds us to it, and set us free, but Jesus. He does this when He pardons us. And if this is so, then it must be true that the pardon of our sins is the greatest benefit that we can receive.

But there is another thing which shows us what a great blessing this pardon is, and that is *the dreadful things that people, who have never heard the joyful sound of the gospel, are willing to suffer in the hope of getting their sins pardoned.* We see this illustrated by some of the cruelties practised by the heathen in the worship of their false gods. The people who have never had the Bible cannot fully understand how dreadful a thing sin is. Still they know enough about it to make them afraid of it, and lead them earnestly to desire to have it pardoned. They know nothing of the precious blood of Jesus which cleanses from all sin. Their religion points out no certaiu way to obtain pardon. And so, when those people are troubled about their sins, the priests tell them to do a great many painful things, not as a *sure* way to obtain pardon, but only in the bare hope that these things may please their gods, and then, *perhaps*, they may pardon their sins.

Sometimes they will make the people walk round the temples of their gods in shoes which have the points of nails sticking through the soles, so that their feet will be kept bleeding at every step. Sometimes they will tell them that they must lie, for days and weeks and months, on beds covered

HEATHENS DOING PENANCE.

over with blunted iron spikes. Sometimes they will cause them to have a hole bored through their tongues, and a small stick thrust through the hole while they make an offering to their god. Sometimes they will have a scaffolding erected before the temple, two or three stories high. At the foot of the scaffold will be placed sacks of wool, flattened out, with spikes of iron sticking through them. Then the people, who wish to please their god, and secure a pardon for their sins, are directed to go up on the scaffolding, stand at the edge of it, spread out their hands, and throw themselves off, so as to fall on the spikes below. Great crowds of people will be watching them, who will clap their hands, and fill the air with shouts as they see the poor creatures fall on those horrible spikes.

Some years ago there was a rich man in India who was troubled about his sins, and wished to get them pardoned. The priest told him that in order to secure this, it was necessary for him to make a *rolling* journey, to a particular temple, in a distant part of India. When he arrived there, he was to set out a plantain tree, and wait till the fruit was ripe, make an offering of the fruit to his god, and then *roll back* again, and then he might hope that his sins would be pardoned. He resolved to do it. So he took his wife and children in a carriage, that they might ride while he was rolling. He used to wrap a strong cloth round his head to protect it from being cut or bruised. Then he would roll himself along the road like a log of wood. Three or four miles a day was as much as he could make. Then he would rest with his family, and start afresh the next day. His son would walk by him and fan him as he rolled along. When he was approaching a village, the people would come out in crowds to meet him, and the musicians would walk before him to the temple in that village. He would roll up to the foot of the idol, and worship him. Then he would spend a few days to rest, and so go rolling on in his long journey. An English missionary met this man when he was still a long way from the temple to which he was going. He had then been *more than seven years* on his journey. Yet he was willing to go rolling on, till he reached the temple, and then to roll all the way back again, with the mere hope that, at last, he might perhaps succeed in getting a pardon for his sins.

But the Bible tells us that " Jesus is exalted to God's right hand, to *give* pardon." The pardon that He gives is free. He asks nothing for it. He gives it " without money, and without price." It is a *full* pardon. It takes away *all* our sins, and blots them out as a cloud, so that God has nothing against us, and we have nothing to fear, either while we live, or when we die; either in this world, or in the world to come. What a blessed thing it is then to hear the joyful sound of the gospel. It is blessed because of the benefits which it brings. The second of these benefits is—*pardon.*

We shall only have time to speak of *one*

more of the benefits which the gospel brings, and this is—HELP.

There is nothing in the world that needs help more than a little infant. It is one of the most helpless of all things. The little duck can plunge into the water, and swim, as soon as it comes out of the shell. The little chicken, too, can run about, at once, and pick up its food. But the little infant can't do anything. It can't feed itself. It can't dress itself. It can't stand, or walk by itself. It needs help for everything. And when we first begin to serve God, or when we become Christians, the Bible compares it to our being born again. Then we are *spiritual infants*. It is the babyhood of our souls then. And we need help for our souls then, just as we do for our bodies, when *they* are in their babyhood. We need the help of Jesus, then, for every thing we try to do. This was what Jesus meant when He said—"without me ye can do nothing." The great difference between Jesus and other teachers is, that they can only tell us what to do, without helping us to do it. But He can do both He can point out the way we ought to walk in, and then give us the help we need to enable us to walk in it. And this is the most important of all things. Of what use would it be to set a beautiful picture down before a blind man, and begin to talk to him about it, unless we could open his eyes and help him to see? Of what use would it be to play on the most perfect musical instrument that ever was, in the presence of a company of deaf men, unless we could unstop their ears, and help them to hear? What would be the use of setting food before a sick man, who had no appetite, unless we could remove his sickness, and help him to get an appetite? And just so I may ask, what use would it be for me to come here, and preach to you every month, to tell you what you ought *not* to do, and what you *ought* to do, and what kind of persons God expects you to be, unless, at the same time I could tell you *where to get the help you need*, to enable you to do what God expects of you? Why, I might as well go out to the cemetery at Laurel Hill, and preach to the dead. You have no more power of your own to change your wicked hearts, and subdue your evil tempers, and love and serve God, than those who are dead and buried, have to come out from their graves, and return to the homes where they once lived. You need help to do this; and not such help as your parents and teachers and friends can give you. You need help from God. And it is a blessed thing to hear the sound of the gospel, because it tells of Jesus, who can give us just such help as we need in trying to serve God. There is one promise in the Bible, about this very view of the character of Christ, which is very sweet and precious. It tells us that He is—"a very *present help* in *every time* of need." It does not matter when, or where you need help, or what you need it for, Jesus can give it you. Let us look at some examples of persons needing help, and finding it in Jesus.

I was reading the other day of a little girl

who was sick. She had to take a dose of very disagreeable medicine.

"Mother, is it bitter, and bad to take?" asked the child, whose name was Amy.

"Yes, my child, it *is* bitter," said her mother, "but not very bad to take, if you make up your mind to take it, like a good girl."

Her mother took her in her arms, and held the glass. She did not coax, or threaten, or promise her pretty things; she wanted her child to be willing to take it for the sake of getting well.

"Wait a minute," said Amy; and clasping her little hands together, she shut her eyes and said, "O my Saviour, will you help a poor little child to take her medicine and be well? Will you please give Amy a mind to do it? Amen."

Then she opened her soft blue eyes, and stretching out her hand, she took the glass, and swallowed the medicine.

A lady had charge of a class of little boys in Sunday school. Every Sunday she used to give the class some subject to think about, and which they were to find texts in the Bible to prove by the next Sunday. One day she gave them this sentence, "Jesus Christ loved little children." The scholars were to write down, on a paper, all the passages they could find to prove this. The next Sunday came. She met her class. There was a little boy in it named Harry. He was very poor, but a bright-eyed little fellow, always very attentive, and his teacher loved him very much.

"Well, Harry," said the teacher, "have you found the verses?"

"Yes, ma'am," said Harry, as he handed the paper. Then he turned to the places which he had marked down in his Bible, and read them. His teacher was surprised to find how very suitable the passages were to prove what had been given to the class. She thought that if the minister of the parish had selected them, they could not have been better chosen. Then she began to think that he must have had somebody to help him, so she said,

"Harry, did any one help you to find these texts?"

"Yes, ma'am," said Harry. His teacher was pleased to find him so ready to acknowledge this, and not want to take the credit to himself. Then she asked herself, 'well, who could have helped him?' She knew that his mother was dead, that his father was a wicked, drunken man, and that he had no brother or sister old enough to help him. Then she said to him.

"Harry, dear, who helped you?"

The little fellow looked right up in her face and said in a moment—"God helped me, ma'am." Before he began to study his lesson, he had kneeled down and prayed to Jesus to help him, and his prayer had been heard, and answered.

One day Haydn, the celebrated musician, was talking with two of his musical friends, about the best way of strengthening and refreshing themselves when they had been singing a great deal, and were very tired. One of them said that nothing helped him like a bottle of wine. The other said that going into lively company was the best thing for him. They asked Haydn what he did. He said he always went into his chamber and engaged in prayer; for that when he was weary, and troubled in his mind, he found that nothing was such a help and comfort to him as prayer to God.

When we read about the martyrs, who were tortured, and burnt, and put to cruel deaths because they would not deny their Saviour, we often wonder to ourselves how it was that they could be so cheerful and happy even while their bodies were burning in the fire. If we just put our finger against the stove, for a moment, when it is red-hot we know very well how badly it pains us. Then how dreadful it must have been to be burnt to death! Yet some of the martyrs went to meet this fearful death as pleasantly as if they had been going to a feast. Sometimes they would hold out their hands in the flames, and sing praises to God while they were burning. How could they do it? *God helped them.* And if he can help men to sing while they are burning, as if the fire did not hurt them at all, then what is there that He cannot help his people to do? Oh, when you want help, for anything, ask Jesus to give it to you. If you want to overcome sins; if you want to resist temptations; if you want to get wicked tempers changed; if you want to be patient in trial and suffering, as Jesus was; if you want to live so as to serve and please God here in this life, and go to heaven when you die—you must pray to Jesus to help you. He has promised to do this. He says in the Bible, "*I will help thee.*" But if we want His help we must pray earnestly for it, and try to help ourselves.

We have spoken of three great benefits which the gospel brings to us, and on account of which it is a blessed thing to hear its joyful sound. What is the first of these benefits? *Knowledge.* What is the second? *Pardon.* What is the third? *Help.*

My dear young friends, let us try to improve this knowledge, and to get this pardon and help for ourselves, and then we shall be truly happy. We shall understand what our text means when it says, "Blessed are the people that know the joyful sound!"

III.

The Blessedness of Considering the Poor.

"Blessed is he that considereth the poor."

PSALM xli. 1.

III.

"Blessed is he that considereth the poor."

PSALM xli. 1.

DID you ever go into a gymnasium? No doubt many of you have been. A gymnasium is a place for taking exercise in. There are a great many different things there to help people who want to take exercise. There are dumb bells, and clubs for swinging round, so as to stretch out the arms. There are ropes and ladders to climb up, and parallel bars, and springing boards to help persons in jumping. There are pullies with heavy weights attached to them, for opening and enlarging the chest; besides a great many other things. Now if we should go into a gymnasium, without ever having seen one before, we should know, from just looking at it, that the person who planned it intended it for exercising the limbs, and promoting the health and strength of those who should use it.

Now the world, in which we live, is like a great gymnasium. It is a place which God has planned, and fitted up with everything that is necessary to exercise the hearts or souls of his people, and to bring into play the right sort of feelings. There are a good many things in the world that God has put here for this very purpose. One of these things is the fact that there are so many poor people in the world. Jesus told his disciples, that there would always be poor people on the earth. Many people wonder why it is so. If you knew a man worth half a million of dollars, whose children were allowed to go in ragged clothing, and to live in a very poor, shabby looking hut, you would think it very strange. Now all the gold and silver, all the precious things, all the property in the world belong to God. Yes, and millions of times more than all *this* world contains. O, how rich our Father in heaven is! And yet how very poor many of His children are!

Why, if our Heavenly Father pleased, He could easily give to you and to me, and to every one of His children ten, or twenty, or fifty thousand dollars a year. And He *would* do it, in a minute, if He saw that it would be best for us. God lets His people be poor, not because he can't make them rich, for this would be a very easy thing for him to do, but because He has good and wise reasons why he wants them to be poor while they live in this world. One of these reasons David taught us when he wrote the words of our text:—"Blessed is he that considereth the poor." There are some things which are a great deal better than money. God's blessing is one of these things. This blessing is connected with *considering* the poor; *i. e.*, with thinking about them, being kind to them, and trying to do them good. This is particularly a Bible Blessing. There are no hospitals, no asylums, or homes for the poor in heathen lands.

Now I wish to speak of *three* reasons why it is a blessed thing to consider the poor.

The first reason is that IT IS LIKE GOD.

David says, "Thou, O God, hast of Thy goodness, prepared for the poor." What wonderful preparation God makes for the poor! He not only provides for poor people, but poor animals too. It says in the Bible that "the lions, roaring after their prey, seek their meat from God. He feedeth the young ravens when they cry." All the beasts of the earth, the birds of the air, and the fishes of the sea, are fed by God. How large a family this is! What different kinds of food they require! But God "*considers*" what they want, and gets it ready for them.

Some travelers lately went up a high mountain, fourteen thousand feet high. It is covered with ice and snow at the top all the year. No men could live up there. Even if they could stand the cold, they could find nothing to eat. But the travelers found some insects living there. God had made the mountain-top a home for them, and He had provided them with plenty of food just such as they needed.

In preparing to lay the wires for the magnetic telegraph to Europe some time since, it became necessary to find out how deep the water in the ocean was, up towards the coast of Greenland. The men who were sounding for this purpose measured in one place where the water was seven thousand feet deep. And yet, even at that great depth—about thirty-five times as far down as the height of Christ Church steeple—they found live shell fish at the bottom of the ocean. And God had not forgotten them. Away down, under all that depth of water, God has prepared them the food they need. God is always considering the poor. When He makes the sun to shine, and the rains to descend, and the dews to distil, He does it, among other reasons, that the grain may grow, and the fruits of the earth may ripen, on which both the rich and poor are dependent for their food.

But then God does more than this. He considers the poor in a special way, and when He knows that those who love Him are suffering for the want of anything, He takes particular pains to send them what they need. Let me show how He sometimes does this.

A poor minister, with a large family depending upon him, was suddenly left without employment in the midst of a severe winter. The last penny had been spent for food, and the last morsel was put upon the table, making a scanty supper for the hungry children. The poor mother went to bed with a sorrowful heart, when she thought that there was not a mouthful of food, in the house, to give the children when they should wake in the morning. The father kneeled down and prayed, earnestly, to God, telling Him their wants, and asking Him to supply them.

But when the morning came, there was nothing in the house. The hungry children cried for food, and their parents could only tell them they had nothing to give.

"Put on the kettle, my dear," said the minister to his wife, "and spread the cloth as usual, and let us trust that God will send us something yet."

She did so. Soon the kettle was boiling—but still there was nothing to eat. The poor distressed father stood by the fire, and looked on his hungry children, while his heart was almost ready to break.

Presently there came a knock at the door. The eldest child opened it, and a gentleman handed him a letter telling him to give it to his father. It was opened, and found to contain several bank notes, with a few lines telling him to use them as he pleased. Very soon a nice breakfast was prepared, and that happy family ate heartily of the good things before them, while their hearts were filled with gratitude to God, who "considers the the poor," and who had heard their prayers, and sent them just what they needed.

They found out afterwards that the gentleman who left the letter, was going out to take a walk before breakfast. Just as he was leaving his house, it came into his mind, all at once, to leave some money at the house of this good minister, and he did so. No doubt God sent His angel to whisper this thought to him. God considered this poor family in their distress, and then He prepared them a supply. And God is doing this, in one way or another, all the time. He never stops giving for a moment. He gives to angels. He gives to men. He gives to all his creatures "life, and breath, and all things." And this is one reason why we should "consider the poor," and try to relieve them all we can : because it is *like God.*

The second reason why we should consider the poor is because WE CAN MAKE THEM HAPPY IN THIS WAY.

And this is what God sent us into the world for. God is doing all he can to make people happy. The Bible tells us that God sent His Son, Jesus, into the world on purpose to bless us, *i. e.*, to make us happy. And when we learn to love Jesus, and try to do those things that please Him, we shall not only be happy ourselves, but we shall be trying to make others happy. And one of the best ways of doing this is by "considering the poor"; by trying to be kind to them, and to help them in their troubles and sorrows.

One day a poor man was going into the counting-house of a very wealthy merchant in New York. As he went in he saw great piles of gold and silver which the clerks were busy in counting. It was in the midst of winter. The poor man thought of his desolate home, and the wants of his family, and, almost without thinking, he said to himself, "Ah! how happy a very little of that money would make me!" The merchant overheard him. "What is that you say, my friend?" he asked. The poor man was confused, and begged to be excused, as he did not intend to say anything. But the kind-hearted merchant wouldn't excuse him, and so the man was obliged to repeat what he had said. "Well, my good fellow," said the merchant, "and how much would it take to make you happy?" "O, I don't know, sir," said he, "but the weather is very cold, and I have no wood; my wife and children are poorly clad, for I have been sick. But we don't want much. I think, sir, about fifteen dollars would get us all we need." "John," said the merchant to his clerk, "count this man out fifteen dollars."

The man's heart was made glad, and he went back to a home that was made glad too.

At the close of the day, the clerk asked the merchant how he should enter in his books the money given to the poor man. He answered: "Say, 'For making a man happy, fifteen dollars.'"

Perhaps that merchant never spent fifteen dollars better in his life.

A great many years ago, not long after the revolutionary war, a benevolent-looking gentleman, dressed in black, and wearing a three-cornered hat, was walking along one of the streets in this city. As he went on, he saw a little boy, poorly clothed, who seemed pinched with hunger. The little fellow seemed as if he wanted to beg, and yet was unwilling to do it. And that was the fact. His poor sick mother had been obliged, for the first time in her life, to send her son out into the streets to beg a little. The gentleman spoke kindly to the child. He took him gently by the hand, and walked on with him. The little fellow told him the sad story of their sorrows:—he told him his father's name; how he had died not long before; how hard his mother had worked to get them bread; how she had been taken sick, and what they had suffered since then.

The gentleman told the child to lead him to their home. On his way there, he stopped at the grocery store, and ordered a supply of things. On entering the house, he saw, in a moment, that it was food the poor woman needed, more than medicine, to make her well. He told her that he was not a regular physician, but he thought he could do something for her that would cure her. He said he would write a prescription, which, if she would send and get, he felt pretty sure would do her good. So he wrote the prescription, and left it on the table. Then he shook hands kindly with the poor woman, spoke a few cheerful words to her, and said he would come and see her again, in a few days, and give her another prescription, if she needed it.

When he was gone, the poor widow looked at the paper, and you may try to imagine what her feelings were when she found that it was an order for a hundred dollars, and signed by the name of GEORGE WASHINGTON! The great, the good, the noble Washington! the man who was always "first in war, first in peace, and first in the hearts of his countrymen," had done this kind act! What an honor it is to belong to a country of which he was the father and the saviour! How pleasant it is to think that the "Bible Blessing" we are now speaking of—the blessing of "considering the poor," and making them happy, belonged to our glorious Washington. What a blessed thing it is to make poor, suffering people happy, as Washington made that sick widow, and her family! It seems to me that if God should send an angel down from heaven to earth, and let him do as he pleased, the angel would want to imitate Washington's example by considering and comforting the poor. Indeed, we know that when Jesus, the Lord of Angels, was here, *this* was what He loved most to do. He " went about doing good."

The second reason why we should consider the poor, is, that *we can make them happy* by doing this.

The third reason why we should do this, is BECAUSE WE DO GOOD TO OURSELVES BY IT.

We may be very sure of this, because God has promised it. Just see what he says in the verse in which our text is found : " Blessed is he that considereth the poor : the *Lord will deliver him in time of trouble.*" And then there is another promise in the Bible which reads thus : " He that hath pity upon the poor, *lendeth to the Lord*, and that which he hath given, will he pay him again." If we lend our money to any one else, we never can be sure of getting it back again; but if we lend it to the Lord, we may be perfectly sure that He will pay us back, and always with good interest.

There is a story told of a good bishop who was very charitable. Once, when he was traveling, some poor people met him, and begged for help. The bishop asked his servant how much money they had with them. He said, "three crowns, sir." "Give them to these poor people," said the bishop. But the servant thought his master was too liberal. So he gave two crowns to the poor people, and kept one to pay for their lodging at night.

Not long after, a certain rich nobleman met the bishop. Knowing how charitable he was to the poor, he ordered his steward to pay two hundred crowns to the bishop's servant for his master's use. The servant was overjoyed, and hastened to tell his master what had happened. "Ah," said the bishop, "if you had only had more faith in God, and given the three crowns to the poor, as I told you, you would have had three hundred crowns now, instead of two hundred."

Thus you see how the bishop was blessed for considering the poor. "That which he paid away, God paid him again." *He did good to himself* by considering the poor.

Two boys applied for a place in a gentleman's store. One was older than the other, and had some experience in the business. He was a gentleman's son, and well-dressed. The other was the only son of a poor widow. His clothes were well mended, but perfectly clean, and his face had quite an honest expression, which was like a letter of recommendation. It seemed most likely that the gentleman's son would get the situation, yet the merchant gave it to the poor widow's son in preference. Now let me tell you what led him to do this.

The two boys came together at the hour appointed, and the merchant was on his door-step at the time. Just then a poor little shivering child crossed the street, and as she stepped on the sidewalk, her foot slipped on the icy stones, and she fell in the half-melted snow. The elder boy laughed at her sorry appearance, with the water dripping from her thin, ragged clothes; but the child began to cry bitterly as she searched for the four pennies she had lost. Willie, the younger boy, hastened to her side, and helped her search for the pennies. Two were found in the snow, the other two were probably in the little icy pool beside the curb-stone. Willie bravely rolled up his sleeve, and plunged his hand down into the water, groping about till one of the missing pennies was found; the other seemed hopelessly lost.

"I'm afraid that can't be found, little girl," said he, pleasantly.

"Then I can't get the bread," sobbed the child, "and mamma and the children will have no supper."

"Here is a penny," said Willie, taking one from a little purse which contained the small stock he had. Then he made haste to wash off his hand in the snow, and dry it on his coarse white handkerchief. The other boy looked on with contempt, and said, "You are a greenhorn in the city, Mister."

But the gentleman who had seen it thought differently. He determined to take Willie in spite of his patched clothes. Thus Willie was "blessed for considering the poor." *He did good to himself* by it. He lent a penny to the Lord, when he gave it to that poor child, and God paid it back to him again.

Nearly half a century ago, before the time of railways, when people traveled in stage-coaches, a coach used to run daily between Glasgow and Greenock, in Scotland. One afternoon, as this coach was going by a place called Bishopton, a lady in the coach saw a little boy walking barefoot along the road. He seemed tired, and suffering with his feet. She asked the driver to take him up and give a seat, and she would pay for it. When they arrived at the inn in Greenock, she inquired of the boy what he had come there for. He said he wished to be a sailor, and hoped some of the captains would take him as a cabin boy. The lady gave him half a crown, and spoke some kind words to him, wishing him success, and charging him not to learn to swear or drink.

Twenty years passed away. The coach was returning to Glasgow one afternoon on the same road. Among the passengers in the stage, was a sea captain ; and when they came near Bishopton, the very spot where the kind lady took up the little boy, the captain saw an old lady on the road, walking slowly, and looking very tired and weary. He asked the coachman to put her in the coach, as there was an empty seat, and he would pay her passage. Soon after, while changing horses, all the passengers got out except the sea captain and the old lady. The lady thanked the captain for his kindness to her, as she was unable to pay for a seat. He said he always felt bound to help weary travelers whenever he could, because when he was a boy, twenty years ago, near this very place, a kind-hearted lady ordered the coachman to take him up, and paid for his seat. "Ah!" said the lady, "I remember that day very well. *I* am that lady, sir; but my lot in life has greatly changed. Then I was very well off; but now I am left quite poor, through the bad conduct of my intemperate son."

"O, I am so glad to meet you again, my good friend," said the captain, shaking her warmly by the hand. "I have been very successful in business, and am going home to live on my fortune; and from this day I shall bind myself and my heirs to pay you twenty pounds" (*i. e.*, a hundred dollars a year), "as long as you live."

This lady "considered the poor," and you see how she was blessed for it. *She did good to herself* at the same time that she made that poor boy happy. She lent her half crown to the Lord, and He paid it her again.

Let me tell you one more story to show how God blesses those who consider the poor, by making their kind actions do good to themselves.

Some time ago, three boys set out to walk

from a village in Holland to the town of Amheim, which was about nine miles from where they lived. The king of Holland was expected to arrive at Amheim, and there was to be a grand procession in honor of his arrival, and the boys resolved to go and see it. This was the reason of their going.

They had not gone very far before they found a little girl, about three years old, sitting under a tree in a field, and crying bitterly. Her dress showed that she belonged to a wealthy family. They asked her to tell them where she lived, but in reply to their questions, she only called on her mamma, and kept on crying. They saw that the poor child was lost. They talked to her, and tried to comfort her a little while. Then two of the boys, whose names were Hans and Gussy, were not willing to stay any longer. They wanted to hurry on to the town, and see the king.

" But we can't leave this child here alone," said Fritz, the other boy.

"Nonsense," said Hans, " she'll find her

way home some how, I daresay. Providence will take care of her."

"But I think Providence has sent us here to take care of her," said Fritz.

"If you stay here much longer," said Gussy, "you'll be too late to see the king."

"King or no king," said Fritz, "I'm not going till I see this child safe."

"Good luck to you then," said the other boys, "we are off." And off they went towards Arnheim.

As soon as they were gone, Fritz began to think what he had better do. He looked all round, and presently he spied a gentleman's house away off from him. "Good," said he, "I'll carry her there, and ask them to take care of her."

"Come away, sissy dear," said he, "and I'll take you to your mamma." Then he lifted her up in his arms, and carried her a little way. But though he was a pretty stout boy, he soon found that she was too heavy for this. So he set her down, and fixed her on his back, with her arms round his neck, after the style that boys call "pig-a-back."

In this way he found he could get on very easily, and the little girl seemed pleased, and began to smile and chuckle.

As soon as Fritz drew near the gentleman's house, a beautifully dressed lady who was coming up the lane, gave a loud cry. Then she ran up to Fritz, and took the child from his back. It was her own child. She kissed it again and again, while tears of joy ran down her cheeks. The child, too, laughed and cried for gladness, and nestled down in her mother's bosom, and clasped her little arms round her neck, as if she was never going to let go of her again.

While this was going on, a gentleman, elegantly dressed, came up from another lane, where he had been hunting for the child. Behind him was the farmer; while from a third lane came the farmer's wife, and the maid-servant, and the man-servant, and the cat and the little dog, all seeming to be excited at the loss of the little girl. They all gathered round the happy mother, and nothing was heard but expressions of gratitude and joy. Pussy purred as loud as she could, and the little dog jumped about and wagged his tail to show how glad he was.

All this time Fritz stood with his cap in one hand and his handkerchief in the other, with which he was wiping off the perspiration from his face. Presently the gentleman took him by the hand and said—

"Ah! my good fellow! what joy you have caused us! Where did you find her?"

"Over yonder in the fir-bush," said Fritz, pointing to the place.

"And did you carry her all that way?" asked her mother. "She was a heavy burden to you, I'm sure, my good boy."

"I often carry a bag of rye to the mill," said Fritz, "and that's heavier, ma'am."

"Take this and buy something for yourself," said the gentleman, offering him a silver coin.

"No, thank you," said Fritz, "I'd rather not take anything."

"Why not?" asked the gentleman.

"Wasn't it my duty, sir, to carry the child home? I'm glad I've found you so soon. I think I can still get to Arnheim in time."

"So you want to go to Arnheim to see the king?" said the gentleman. "Very good. We are just going there ourselves. Will you sit on the box with the coachman?"

Of course, Fritz had no objection to this. While the horses were getting harnessed, the gentleman took Fritz into the house, and gave him some cake and wine.

Soon the carriage was ready. The gentleman and his lady, with the nurse and baby got in, and Fritz mounted up on to the box with the driver. What a pleasure it was to him! He had never sat so high in his life. And what speed! The horses seemed almost to fly along the road. In about an hour after starting, they overtook the two boys, just before entering Arnheim. They looked dusty and tired.

"Hallo! old fellows, how do you do? Hurrah!" cried Fritz, swinging round his cap as the carriage flew past. It drove straight on under all the flags and wreaths that hung over the streets.

The evening of that day, the three boys were walking home by moonlight. "Did you see anything, Gussy?" said Hans. "Not a thing," said Gussy. "There was such a crowd I couldn't even see the king's carriage; and I'm so hungry I can hardly keep from biting my tongue."

"So am I," said Hans. "I was obliged to stand all the time behind a big fat farmer, who was about a yard above me. Did you see anything, Fritz?"

"Didn't I, though?" said Fritz. "I sat on the top of the box of that gentleman's carriage, whose little child I carried home in the morning. I saw the king and the guard of honor. I saw all the soldiers, and the royal carriages, and everything. And every now and then the gentleman handed me up some nice cake, and before I left he made me take this," said Fritz, holding up a handsome silver watch.

You may imagine how the boys felt. When Fritz went home that night he understood what David meant when he said, "Blessed is he that considereth the poor." He found it was a blessed thing because it had done good to himself.

Thus we have spoken of three reasons why it is a blessed thing to consider the poor. The *first reason is, that it is like God;* the second is—*it makes them happy;* the third is—*it does good to ourselves.*

Our sermon to-day is about something which we can all begin to do. It is not for rich, only, but for the poor, too; not for the old, only, but for the young, also.

A gentleman, near London, once went to visit a poor woman who was sick. When he entered the room he saw a little girl kneeling at her bedside, who immediately went out. He asked the sick woman who the child was? "Oh! sir," said she, "it is a little angel who often comes in to read the Bible to me, to my great comfort, and who has just left sixpence with me." On inquiring further, he found that the little girl was poor herself, and that the sixpence left with the sick woman had been given to the child for a reward. She began to practice on the text with only sixpence. How very few there are but what have that much!

But considering the poor doesn't always mean giving them money It often means, speaking kindly to them, and showing that we feel sympathy for them.

A young lady in New York had gone out to take a walk. She forgot to take her purse with her, and had no money in her pocket. Presently she met a little girl with a basket on her arm. "Please, Miss, will you buy something from my basket?" said the little girl, showing a variety of book marks, watch cases, needle books, etc.

"I'm sorry I can't buy anything to-day," said the young lady, "but I haven't got a cent with me. Your things look very pretty." She stopped a moment, and spoke a few kind words to the little peddler. And then, as she passed on, she said, again, "I'm very sorry I can't buy anything from you to-day."

"Oh! Miss," said the little girl, "you've done me just as much good as if you had. Most persons that I meet, say, 'Get away with you.' But you have spoken kindly to me, and I feel a heap better."

That was considering the poor. How little it costs to do that! Let us learn to speak kindly and gently to the poor and the suffering. If we have nothing else to give, let us at least give them our sympathy

"Speak gently, kindly, to the poor,
Let no harsh tone be heard;
They have enough they must endure,
Without an unkind word.
Speak gently, for 'tis *like the Lord*,
Whose accents meek and mild,
Bespoke him as the Son of God,
The gracious, holy *Child*."

IV.

How Jesus Blesses Men.

"Men shall be blessed in Him." PSALM lxxii. 17.

IV.

"Men shall be blessed in Him." PSALM lxxii. 17.

WHAT an interesting thing it is to see a little infant! How helpless it is! It looks so innocent, so sweet, that we can't help loving it. And when we stand by its cradle and gaze on it, we are ready to say—"Well, this is the *beginning* of another life." Be·ore that child lived as an infant it had never lived at all. This is true of all the infants ever born except one. 1864 years ago an infant was born in Bethlehem, who was different from all other infants, in this respect. He had a manger for his cradle. But when he began to live, as an infant, *that* was *not* the beginning of *his* life. He had lived before he was born into this world. He had lived, not as a man,—not as an angel,—but as God, in heaven. He had lived, not fifty years,—not a hundred years,—but thousands and millions of years. He had lived before there was a single star in yonder sky: before there was an angel in heaven. He had *always* lived. There never was a beginning to his life.

But when he was born into this world as an infant, he began to live in a new way. Before that, as I said, he had lived as God. But when that remarkable baby was born in Bethlehem, he began to live as man. What a wonderful thing this was! It was the most wonderful thing that ever happened in this world. The great God of heaven was born as a little infant! *How* could this be? I don't know. I can't tell you how it was. But it is just as true, as that you are alive. Suppose that all the water in the ocean were pressed together so that it could be put into the hollow of my hand. How wonderful that would be! But still it wouldn't be half so wonderful, as that God, who made all things, should become a little child. We never can get through wondering over this. It is not surprising that the prophet Isaiah, when speaking about it, should have said that "His name should be called *wonderful.*" A great many things were said about Him before He was born. One of these is spoken of in our text. "*Men shall be blessed in Him.*" King David spoke these words more than a thousand years before the birth of Jesus. It tells us in the New Testament that God sent His Son into the world *to bless men.* Acts iii. 26. And as we have our anniversary this year on Christmas, the day which celebrates the birth of Jesus, it will be a subject suitable to the day, if our sermon is about *the way in which He blesses people:* or, *what Jesus does for people to make them blessed.*

Everybody in the world receives some blessing from Jesus. The blessings He obtained for us are so numerous that even the poor heathen, who have never heard of His name, have received some of His blessings. But I wish to speak of what Jesus does for His own people, for those who love and serve

Him, to make them blessed. I will mention *three* things which Jesus does to bless them.

The first thing He does for them is to MAKE THEM WISE.

It is a great thing to be wise. But people may be wise in many different ways. Some men are wise to make money, and others are wise to get honor. Some men are wise to build houses, and others are wise to build ships. Some are wise to cure diseases, and others are wise to make interesting books, or to invent curious machines, that no one else ever thought of. Some are wise as generals to win battles, and others are wise as rulers to govern states, or nations. Some are wise to do good, and others are wise to do evil. But I do not mean any of these ways, when I speak of Jesus making people wise. The way in which He blesses people is by making them wise so serve God—wise to save their souls—wise to get to heaven. This is the only true wisdom. The Bible says this "wisdom is the *principal* thing." "It is more precious than rubies," and "He that findeth this wisdom is happy, or blessed."

Suppose that you and I had to go on a voyage round the world. It will take us three years to make the voyage. We can get no supply of provisions after we have once started. The vessel is to sail in ten days. That is all the time allowed us to lay up the provisions, and clothing, and other things necessary for the voyage. But, suppose, that instead of beginning at once to get a good supply of fresh water, and flour, and rice, and potatoes, and bread, and meat, and tea, and coffee, and sugar, and such things as we should want, we spend those ten days in chasing butterflies, and flying kites, or in dancing, and singing, and going into company. At last the ten days are gone. The Captain sends us a summons to come on board the ship. We are obliged to go. The anchor is raised. The sails are unfurled. The ship has started on her long voyage. But we have made no preparation for it. Would it be wise for us to act so? O, no;

it would be very foolish. But suppose, that instead of flying kites and chasing butterflies, we had spent those ten days, in sleeping or in reading, or in looking after our trade, or business, would that have made it any better? No, not a bit. The only wise thing for us to have done, would have been to prepare for that long voyage. Whatever else we might have done till we were ready for that voyage would have been folly. If any body had wanted to bless us, as persons who had a long voyage before us, the only way of doing it would have been by making us wise to get ready.

And this is just our situation. We have a long voyage before us. We start upon this voyage when we die. When once started we never can come back to get what we want. And there is no place where we can get supplies after starting. God has sent us here to get ready. Jesus has come to bless us in making us wise to prepare for this voyage. He says to all people—"Seek *first* the kingdom of heaven." This means—get ready for heaven before you do anything else. But when we see people attending to their business, to amusements, or to pleasure, while their hearts are not changed, their sins are not pardoned; while they do not love Jesus, and they have made no preparation for that long, long voyage on which they are soon to start, we need not wonder to find that the Bible calls them—*fools.* They are flying kites, and chasing butterflies, instead of preparing for their voyage. They forget their souls, and think only about their bodies.

Not long ago, a mother was putting her little girl to bed. The child was about three years old. Her mother had been kneeling down by her bedside, and teaching her to repeat the Lord's prayer. After finishing it she rose up and was going out of the door, when the little girl cried out,

"O, mother! you have forgotten *my soul!*"

"What do you mean, my child?" asked the mother.

"Why—

"Now I lay me down to sleep,
I pray the Lord *my soul* to k ep;
And if I die before I wake,
I pray the Lord *my soul* to take."

She only meant to say that her mother had omitted one of her prayers. But her words seemed to mean a great deal more than this. "You have *forgotten my soul!*" O, how many boys, and girls and men and women, are just doing this—*forgetting their souls!* But Jesus teaches his people to think about their souls, and get them saved. The first way in which he blesses them is *by making them them wise.* He makes them wise about their souls.

The second way in which he blesses them is by making them STRONG.

I said, a little while ago, that there are different ways of being wise, and so now I may say there are different ways of being strong. Sometimes people are strong *in body.* Samson was strong in this way.

What wonderful power he had! He could take hold of a lion and tear its jaws asunder with his own hands. He could pull up the huge gates of a city with the posts and bars, and carry them all away on his shoulders. He could kill a thousand men with the jaw-bone of an ass. He could take hold of the pillars of a great temple, and bend them like young twigs, and tumble the whole building down, just as easily as a child can knock down a house of blocks, or cards.

Some people are *strong in mind.* They can do a wonderful deal of thinking with great ease. Napoleon Bonaparte was so strong in mind, was such a great thinker, that he could keep six persons writing, and could think for them all just as fast as they could write

And then some persons are *strong in soul.* I mean by this that they have power or strength to do what is right, and to resist what is wrong. This is the strength that Jesus gives to His people. I don't mean to say that He doesn't give the other kinds of strength too, for all the strength of any kind that people have comes from Him. But I mean that strength of soul is the best kind of strength, and Jesus blesses His people by giving them this. And this strength is very important, because there is so much wickedness in the world, that unless we are made strong in this way we cannot keep from sinning. Without this strength we shall be just like wax, in the hands of bad people, and they will twist us into any shape they please. How much of this strength Daniel had, when he wouldn't stop praying, even though the king threatened to put him into the den of lions! And how much of this strength Shadrach, Mesheck, and Abednego had, when they would rather be thrown into the fiery furnace than worship the idol of the king of Babylon. A soul without strength is like a body without a back-bone. The back-bone runs through the body, like a pillar, or column, and supports it. If we had no back-bones our bodies would all fall in a heap, like an empty bag. We couldn't stand, or walk,

SHADRACH, MESHECH AND ABEDNEGO BEFORE THE KING.

or work without them ; but with them, we can stand, and lift, and do what we please. It is a good thing to have a strong body, but it is a great deal better to have a strong soul.

"Mother," said a little boy, as he came home from school one day—"I'm sure you would like Tom Ashton, in our school."

"Why so, Willie?" asked his mother.

"Because, when the boys want him to play truant, or swear, or tell lies, or do anything that is wrong, he gives them such a rousing—no!"

Tom Ashton had back-bone in his soul. Jesus had made him strong. It is a great blessing to be able to give "a rousing no" when we are tempted to do wrong.

Some years ago, a boy, who was left without father or mother, went to New-York to get a situation in a store. He was alone, and without friends, in that great city. He soon became acquainted with some bad boys. Finding that they smoked cigars and drank liquor, whenever they could get it, because they thought it was manly, he learned to do so too. His name was Charles Wilson.

Charles had a pretty good education. In looking over the newspaper, one day, he saw an advertisement that a merchant in Pearl Street, wanted a boy of his age, and he went to the place, at once, to try and get the situation.

"Walk into the office, my lad," said the gentleman, "and I'll attend to you directly."

When he had waited on his customer, he came into the office, and took a seat near Charles, and looked at him, attentively, for a moment. While doing this, he saw a cigar sticking out of the corner of his coat-pocket. That was enough.

"My boy," said he, "I want a smart, honest, faithful lad; but I see you smoke cigars. Boys who smoke sôon learn to drink. I find from your breath, that you have been drinking, too. You can go. You won't do for me."

Poor Charles hung down his head ashamed, and left the store. He hurried back to his lodging-place, and throwing himself on the bed, he cried and sobbed as if his heart would break. He thought of his mother's last words, and how he had neglected them. Upon her death-bed she called him to her side, and placing her thin, white hand on his head, she said :—"Charlie, my dear boy, I'm going to leave you. You know what misery and disgrace your father brought upon us before his death, by drinking. I want you to promise me, before I die, that you will never taste a drop of the terrible poison that killed your father. Promise me this, and be a good boy, Charlie, and I shall die happy."

The scalding tears trickled down Charlie's cheeks, as he promised always to remember his mother's words, and never to drink any intoxicating liquors. But he had broken his promise, made to his dying mother, and now he was feeling the sad effects of his fault. He thought of the text, "Be sure your sins will find you out." "I'm sure my sin has found me out," he said to himself. But he resolved not to go on in this bad way. His mother had taught him where to look for help and strength. So he rose from the bed and kneeled down, and asked God to forgive him the sin he had committed, in breaking his word, and getting into those bad habits. He asked God to make him strong to resist temptation, and to do right. And he promised, by the help of God, never to smoke another cigar, or drink another drop of liquor.

Then he washed his face, and went straight back to the merchant.

"Sir," said he, "you very properly sent me away this morning, for the bad habits I had been guilty of; but sir, I have neither father nor mother, nor any friends in this city. And though I have not done what I ought to have done, and have forgotten the advice of my poor dying mother, and have broken the promise I made her, yet I have made a solemn vow, by the help of God, never to taste another drop of liquor, or smoke another cigar; and O, sir, if you'll only try me, it's all I ask."

The merchant was so pleased with the manly decision and energy of the boy, that he employed him at once. And he never had reason to regret it. At the end of five years, Charles Wilson became a partner in the business, and is now a wealthy man. Jesus gave him strength of soul to resist temptation, and to do what is right. The second way in which He blesses people is by *making them strong.*

I wanted to show how Jesus blesses his people by making them *rich.* I do not mean rich in gold and silver, but rich in better things. But there will not be time, so I pass this by, and go on to show, *that the third way in which Jesus blesses his people is* BY MAKING THEM GOOD.

No persons in this world can be good until Jesus makes them so. Sometimes we hear parents, and teachers, and even ministers, when talking to children, tell them, "that Jesus won't love them unless they are good;

that Jesus only loves good children." But this is all wrong. It is not what the Bible teaches us. We read in the Bible that—"Jesus Christ came into the world to save"—not good people, but—"sinners." Jesus said himself, while He was on earth—"I came not to call the *righteous*,"—that is, good people,—"but *sinners* to repentance." He said again—"Him that cometh unto me I will in no wise cast out." He didn't say, I won't cast him out if he is good—but I won't cast him out however bad he may be; "though his sins be as scarlet, and though they be red as crimson," I won't cast him out. Paul said that he was the "chief of sinners," and yet as soon as he came to Jesus he was pardoned, and saved. Paul did not try to *make himself good* and then come to Jesus, but he came to Jesus while he was "the chief of sinners," that *He* might make him good. We can't make ourselves good. No one else can make us good. Jesus *alone* can do this for us. He blesses men, and women, and children, whose hearts are full of sin, by taking their sins away, and making them good.

A little girl, whose name was May Davis, came bounding into her father's library, one day. She threw her arms round his neck, and said—

"My dear papa, I'm so very glad that I am your little girl! For to-day I walked home with Fanny Vale, to see her little kitten; and Mr. Vale was so cross to Fanny, he scolded her for being late, when indeed she couldn't help it, and said it was a shame for a girl ten years old to play with a cat. I know I am often very naughty, papa, but I should be ten times worse if Mr. Vale were my father. Oh! I'm so very glad that I am your little girl."

"How did your friend Fanny behave," asked Mr. Davis, as he kissed his little daughter. "Did she answer back angrily?"

"No indeed," said May. "Fanny behaved beautifully—a thousand times better than I should have done. She told her father she was very sorry to be so late, and then putting down the pretty little kitten, she asked if there was anything she could do for him. I don't see how she could be so good, do you, papa?"

"Yes, my dear," said Mr. Davis, "for I know whose little girl Fanny is, and I only wish my little girl was a child of the same Father."

"Indeed I wouldn't like to have Fanny's father for mine," said May, "and I don't see why you should wish such a thing either."

"About a year ago, Fanny gave her heart to Jesus, and now she is God's little girl; and that is what I mean," said Mr. Davis.

"God's little girl?" said May thoughtfully; "and does He keep her from being oftener naughty, and is that why she is always so happy?"

"Yes, darling; that is it," said Mr. Davis.

"Then papa," whispered May, leaning her

head on his shoulder, "I wish—I wish that I was God's little girl too."

"He would love to have you for His child," replied her father, "and will make you His now, if you will only ask Him."

"But I don't know how," said May, looking up sadly, "and besides I am not half good enough to be God's little girl."

"Jesus says—'Suffer *little children* to come unto me,'" said her father; "He does not say suffer *good* little children, but *all* children, no matter how naughty, if they only wish to be good. He will take my little daughter's sinful heart away, and make her holy, and good, if she will only ask Him."

"But is Fanny really *God's* little girl?" asked May. "Why, she loves to laugh and play just like other children, and always seems so merry. Now I thought that when little girls became so very religious, they always looked grave, and didn't care to play, as I do. I knew they would be happier when they came to die, but I never thought they would be happier now."

"My dear May, do you remember the time last summer when you were lost in the woods?" asked her father.

"Yes, indeed," said the child, "I never can forget that day, nor how I cried till you came and found me."

"Well, my dear, did you enjoy the beautiful flowers, and the birds that sang so sweetly in the trees, better when you were lost, and wandering all alone, or when I had found you, and we were walking home together hand in hand?"

"Oh! after you found me, to be sure," cried May, "for then I felt so safe and happy that the flowers and birds seemed a thousand times more beautiful than ever before."

"And just so it is with little Fanny," said Mr. Davis, "once she was lost and wandering far away from the path which leads to Heaven; but now she has an Almighty Father, who is always near, who is keeping her from harm, and guiding her to a bright home in heaven. Would you expect such a little girl to be always grave and sad?"

"No indeed, I should expect her to be just like Fanny,—very, very happy. And papa, I mean to ask God, before I go to sleep, if he won't make me His little girl for Jesus' sake. It will make me so happy to think that I belong to Him."

Now if little May kept her promise, and prayed earnestly to Jesus to make her His little girl, we may be sure that He heard her, and made her to know, and feel, that He blesses people by making them good.

"Mamma," said a little girl to her mother one day, "won't you tell me how I can *be good inside?*"

"What do you mean?" asked her mother.

"Why, I mean that I don't have right feelings in my heart. Papa calls me a good girl, and so does Aunty, and most everybody; but I'm *not* good at all."

"I'm very sorry," said the mother.

"And so am I,"—said Kitty. "But I

know my heart is very wicked. Why, mother when I was dressed to ride yesterday, and the carriage came to the door, you remember papa said there was no room for me. Well, I went into the house, and when you came back, Aunty told you I had been very good about it. But she didn't know. I didn't say anything to her, but I went upstairs, and though I didn't cry, *I thought very wicked things.* I kicked the cushion about because I was so vexed, and I wished the carriage would upset, and the horse would run away!"

And Kitty ended, as she had begun, by saying—"Oh! Mamma, won't you tell me *how I can be good inside?*"

Now there are a great many children and grown people too, who are like Kitty. They keep their lips from *saying* bad things, but they can't keep their hearts from thinking and feeling what is bad. They can be good *outside,* but they can't be good inside. They can stop the stream from running on, but they can't stop the fountain from flowing out.

If we want to have the fountain stopped—if we want to be *good inside*, we must get our hearts changed. And Jesus only, can do this. He says in the Bible, "A new heart will I give them, and a new spirit will I put within them." When Jesus undertakes to make people good, He always begins with the heart. When that is made good, then we are good inside. If you can make a fountain pure, then you may be very sure that the streams which flow out from it, will be pure also.

Sometime ago I went to the Navy-Yard, to see one of the big ships our government was building there. The friend who was showing me about, asked me if I knew where they first went to work in building a ship? I said no. "Well," says he, "the first piece of timber that is laid is the middle of the keel; and all the rest is built up on that." Now the center of the keel is the very middle of the ship. "Ah!" I thought to myself, when

I heard this—"that is just what Jesus does, when He is going to build a Christian. He begins at the heart. He makes that good first, and then, by degrees, He makes all the rest good too. He makes his people "good inside" first; and then He makes them good outside afterwards.

"Men shall be blessed in Him."

We have spoken of three things that Jesus does to His people to make them blessed. What is the first? *He makes them wise.* What is the second? *He makes them strong.* What is the third? *He makes them good.*

How thankful we should be that Jesus has been into our world!

He came to bless us all. If He had not come we never should have had any true wisdom, or strength, or goodness. All these blessings we owe to Him. What reason then we have to be glad that Jesus came into our world! The birth of Jesus made the angels glad in heaven, although He did not come to bless them. But He did come to bless us. Then let us be glad, and rejoice on account of His birth. But the best way of showing our thankfulness is to ask Him to bless us by making us wise, and strong, and good. What a very happy thing it will be for us, if, like little May, we pray to Jesus to make us His children. That will make us happy not only at Christmas, but all through the year.

And what a pleasant thing it is that we should bring an offering to Jesus to-day! The wise men brought their offering to Him, as He lay in the manger. We may bring ours to Him, as He sits on His throne. Jesus did not give money to us; He gave Himself. He shed His blood for us. Shall we not freely give whatever He asks of us to show our love to Him, and help to send the blessings of His gospel to those who are without them?

I was reading lately about a poor cottager in England who seemed to have the right feeling on this subject. She had a number of bee-hives. They were very profitable, as she made a sovereign a year—that is, twenty shillings, or five dollars—out of each of them. A little book fell into her hands about the heathen. It showed how Jesus died for them, how He wanted them all to have the gospel, and wanted all who loved Him to help in sending it to them. And then it put this question—"Shall we refuse to give our money to this good object?" "No," she said, as if the book were talking to her—"I won't, for one." Then she set apart two of her hives, the money from which was to be sold for the missionary cause. In six months she had twenty shillings, which she took to her minister. Knowing how poor she was, he said to her—"Surely, my friend, you can't afford as much as this." She looked at him a moment, and then said—"The Lord hath need of it, Sir—*I must afford it.*"

Jesus came from heaven to bless us. We *are* blessed in Him. Let us try all we can to send the same blessings to others.

V.

The Blessedness of being a Christian.

"Thou shalt be blessed above all people." DEUT. vii. 14.

V.

"Thou shalt be blessed above all people." DEUT. vii. 14.

THIS was spoken to the Jews. They are in many respects the most wonderful nation that ever existed. When we think of all that God has done for them, we see how true it is that they have been "blessed above all people." How wonderful their deliverance from Egypt was! They were a nation of slaves there, just as the negroes in our southern States used to be. God sent Moses to Pharaoh, king of Egypt, to tell him to set the people free, and let them go. Pharaoh said he wouldn't do it. God said He would make him do it. And so He did. He sent the most dreadful plagues upon Egypt, one after another, that ever visited any people. The water in their wells and streams was all turned into blood; the land was filled with swarms of flies, with frogs, and lice, that came into their houses, and covered their beds, and chairs, and tables, and every thing. An army of locusts invaded the land, and ate up every green thing in it. Then there was a fearful disease that destroyed all their cattle;—there were dreadful lightnings, and thunders, and hail-storms, such as had never been known before. And at last, one awful night, just in the middle of the night, all at once, the oldest child in every family died. There was not a house through all the land in which there was not one person dead. There never was such a night as that in Egypt. The people thought they were all going to die at once. Pharaoh was frightened almost out of his senses. He let the people go, that very night. And then how wonderful the things were that God did for the Israelites in the wilderness! He opened up a way for them right through the sea. He spread out a cloud to cover them from the great heat of the sun. He sent a wonderful fiery, cloudy pillar to go before them, all through the wilderness, where there were no roads, to show them the right way. He rained them down bread from heaven, every morning, for forty years. He made a stream of water gush out from a rock, and follow them all through that sandy desert wherever they went. How wonderful all this was!

And then when God brought them to the land of Canaan, what wonderful things He did for them there! He had a tabernacle or temple among them. There He used to come, and speak to them, and tell them what He wanted them to do. He was their king. He governed and protected them. He sent His prophets among them to preach to them, and tell them all about Jesus, the great Saviour, who was going to come among them. While all the other nations in the world were worshipping idols, they were worshipping the true God. They knew the way to heaven when no other people knew it. And thus, you see, how well it might be said of them that they were "blessed above all people."

And this is not all either. The Bible

teaches us that though the Jews are now scattered among all nations, yet God will gather them into their own land again. Jerusalem will be the chief city in the world, greater in its influence and importance than New York, Paris, or London, and the Jews will be the most honored and distinguished nation in the world.

But some of you may say, "Well, we are not Jews, and if the promise of the text *only* applies to them, what good will it do us to talk about it?" Very true, but this promise does not refer *only* to the Jews. It refers to Christians as well. It refers to all the friends of Jesus. It is true of all who love and serve our glorious Saviour, that they are "blessed above all people." The subject of our sermon to-day is—*The blessedness of being a Christian.* There are so many things to say on this subject that there won't be time to say them all in one sermon. We must have another sermon on this text, next month, if we live, in order to get through. But I wish now to speak of *four* things in which it is true of real Christians that they are "blessed above all people."

In the first place they are so—in THEIR NAMES.

And when I speak of the names of Christians, I don't mean the names by which men call them, but the names which God gives to them. If you should take a list of the names of the Christians belonging to this church, you would see no difference between them and the names of those who are not Christians. Among them both you would find a great many Smiths, and Browns, and Jones, and such like.

But if we look into the Bible we shall find a wonderful difference between the names or titles of those who are *not* Christians, and of those who *are*. Where God speaks of those who are not Christians, He calls them "fools,"—"wicked ones,"—"children of wrath,"—"cursed children,"—"enemies of God,"—"a perverse and crooked generation,"—"serpents, a generation of vipers."

What a dreadful thing it is to think of the great and good Lord of heaven calling any persons by such names as these! And then, after looking at these, how pleasant it is to turn and look at the names which God gives, in the Bible, to his own people, to all who love and serve Jesus! He calls them "His beloved,"—His "dear children,"—"the excellent of the earth,"—His "chosen ones in whom His soul delighteth,"—"His lambs,"—His "treasure,"—His "jewels,"—"the sons and daughters of the Lord Almighty." Jesus calls His people by all these sweet names now. But hereafter, He says they shall be called by "a name better than of sons and daughters; even by a new name, which the mouth of the Lord shall name." If I am really a Christian, I cannot tell what the name is by which I shall be called in heaven. But I know it will be a *new* name. It will be a beautiful name, fit for that glorious place, and the holy, happy company that will be there. And when we think of the precious names by which Jesus calls his people now, and the still more precious names by which He will call them hereafter, we may well say of Christians that they are "blessed above all people." In their *names* they are thus blessed.

But secondly, they are "blessed above all people IN THEIR DRESS.

I don't mean the dress of their bodies, but the dress of their souls. Christian people wear the same kind of dress for their bodies that others do, but they wear a very different kind of dress for their souls. We don't know what the soul is. We only know that it is that strange thing in us, which thinks, and loves, and which will live forever. When our body dies, we know that the soul leaves the body, and goes out from it. We can't see it when it goes. We don't know how the soul looks, or what the form or shape of the soul is. Perhaps it looks just like the body. Perhaps it has the same form and appearance as the body, only it is not heavy, or solid like the body. If this is so, then, if we could see the soul of some dear friend, who has died and gone to heaven, we should know it in a moment, just as easily as we should know the body of that friend. And there is a particular kind of dress for the soul, just as there is for the body. We read in the Bible that St. John saw the souls of some of the people of Christ who had died. They were in heaven, when he saw them, standing before the throne of God. And when he saw those souls they were all clothed. Yes, and their clothing was all alike. They were clothed in garments that had been washed and made white for them by Jesus, their Saviour. The Bible tells us of a robe, or garment, or dress, that Jesus puts on the souls of his people when they become Christians, that is, when their hearts are changed, when they repent of their sins, and believe in Him. This is spoken of, as a white dress, or robe. It is like that which Jesus himself wore when He was on the Mount of Transfiguration. Three of his disciples were with Him then. They saw Him while He was transfigured, and they have told us how He looked. His face was shining, like the sun, and his garments were white as snow, so as nobody on earth could whiten them. What a blessed thing it is to have this dress on! There are only two kinds of dresses for the souls of people spoken of in the Bible. One of these is this beautiful white dress which Jesus gives to His people. The other is one which every body, who is not a Christian, must wear. It is spoken of in the Bible, as made of "filthy rags." It is stained, and polluted, and dreadful to look at. If we are Christians, if we really love Jesus, we shall wear the white garment which He gives to His people. If we are not Christians, this garment of "filthy rags" is the only one our souls will ever have to wear. When we die, and our souls go into the presence of God, they will have nothing upon them but those "filthy rags." O, how much ashamed we shall feel! How totally unfit we shall be to go among the white-robed company in heaven! And yet we shall never be able to get rid of those rags there. We shall never be able to get any other dress for our souls to wear.

But if we *are* Christians, if we really love and serve Jesus, then our souls will wear the same robe that Jesus wears Himself. This is the most beautiful dress that ever was. Jesus made it Himself for His people to wear. Nobody else will wear it but them. It will be more beautiful than the dress of the angels. The Bible says it will be "of wrought gold, *all glorious within*." This dress is so beautiful that even God loves to look at it. It will never grow old. It will never wear out. It will never get soiled, or torn. It will be always new, and beautiful.

How true it is that real Christians are "*blessed above all people*." They are so in their dress.

But thirdly—they are so in THEIR RELATIONS.

Persons who have relations who are rich, or great, or honorable, are very fond of thinking about them. If you lived in England.

where there is a queen and a class of people who are called the nobility, i. e. who are earls, and lords, and dukes, you would be apt to feel a little proud if the queen were your aunt, or cousin, or if some great lord or duke was a relation of yours. Almost every body would feel so, more or less. But if you are a Christian, if you really love Jesus, you are much better off than this. You have richer and more honorable relations than if Queen Victoria were your aunt, or sister, or mother, or, than if the Duke of Brunswick, or of Marlborough, were your first cousin. If you are a Christian, God is your father. You belong to God's family. That is the richest, and the best, and the most honorable family, in this world, or in all the universe. Jesus is your elder brother. Heaven is your home. The angels of heaven are all your relations—they are, as it were, your first cousins. And they are very kind, useful sort of cousins too. They are all the time waiting upon you, and trying to do you good. The Bible tells us "they are all ministering spirits"—that means, a kind of servants—to those who love Jesus. Now if this is so, then if we are true Christians, we have more cause to feel—(I will not say proud;—Oh, no, no, not proud,—but)—*thankful*, on account of our relations, than if we were connected by birth, or by marriage, with the highest nobility in the world.

I was reading lately of a very good answer made by a little boy in England, who afterwards became a very distinguished minister of the gospel. One of his schoolmates was boasting, one day, about the number of rich and noble relations that he had. Then he asked the future minister "if there were any *lords* in his family?" "Yes," said the little fellow, "I know there is *one* at least, for I have often heard my mother say, that the *Lord* Jesus Christ is our elder brother."

And when we are in trouble, or distress, what a real comfort it is to have a relation who is able and willing to help us!

Some years ago a poor Austrian officer who was very sick, arrived at a town in Germany which was celebrated for its baths; and crowds of sick people were constantly coming there, with the hope of being cured of their various diseases.

The officer seemed very feeble, and it was not likely that he would live very long. He applied for lodging at several of the hotels, but they wouldn't take him in, because they were afraid he might die in the house. Presently he came to the last hotel where he could hope to get a room, but he was told again that there was none vacant. The poor soldier was greatly distressed. He knew not what to do. But just then a gentleman who was living in the hotel, and who had heard the answer given by the landlord, stepped forward, and said—

"This officer is a relation of mine, and I will share my room with him. He may have my bed, and I can sleep on the sofa."

The landlord couldn't make any objection to this, and so the poor sick soldier was carried to the room of the gentleman who had claimed him as a relation. When he had rested a few moments, and recovered his strength a little, his first question was—

"May I ask your name, my kind friend? How are you related to me? On which side? —through my father, or my mother?"

"I am related to you," said the gentle man, "through our Lord Jesus Christ, who has taught me that every suffering man is my brother, and that I should do to him as I would like to have him do to me."

How kind and pleasant that was! This is just the way in which Jesus would have us all act. And this is just the way in which He is acting all the time to His people, who are His poor relations. He tells us all to "call on Him in the day of trouble, and He will hear us." He is called in the Bible the "brother born for adversity," "the friend that sticketh closer than a brother!"

And the best thing about the Christian's relations is that he can never lose them. The Bible tells us that "nothing can separate us from the love of Christ." Jesus says to His relations that He "will never leave them, nor forsake them." The dearest relations that we have, in this world, are sure to be separated from us by death. And sometimes this separation comes very suddenly, and unexpectedly.

Some years ago there was a family by the name of Winslow, living on the Isle of Wight in England. The family consisted of Mr. and Mrs. Winslow, and one little girl called Lilly. Mr. Winslow had come over to this country to buy a farm, intending, when he had got it all in nice order, to go back and bring his family over to live on the farm. He had written to his wife that every thing was ready, and that he hoped to be at home about, Christmas. But Christmas came, and went without *his* coming. Day after day, and week after week passed by, but still he did not come. His family became very anxious about him, till at last, the sad, sad tidings reached them, one day, that the vessel had been wrecked, and all on board, except three sailors, were drowned. What a dreadful blow that was to Mrs. Winslow and her little daughter! *That* day was the saddest day they had ever known. We can imagine what their sorrow was over their great loss.

Well, at the close of the first day of their affliction, little Lilly kneeled down by her mother's side to say her prayers, as she was accustomed to do. Her mother was weeping, and the tears were streaming down Lilly's own cheeks, as she tried, between her sobs, to say the words she had been used to say from the time she had learned to speak. Presently, almost before she knew it, she found herself saying—"God bless my dear father." Her poor mother uttered a loud cry. "O, Lilly, my darling," she said, "don't say that any more. You have *no father* now." This stopped the poor child. She didn't know what to say next. But, as she had always been in the habit of finishing with the Lord's prayer, she thought she would use that. So she began with those sweet and tender words—"*Our Father who art in heaven.*" How beautiful those words seemed to Lilly then! She thought she had never understood their meaning, or felt how sacred they were, as she did that night. She stopped awhile. Then she said them over again. She said them the third time—"Our Father who art in heaven." Then she looked up into her mother's sorrowing face, and said—"Oh! Mother we have a Father yet. God is our Father. Jesus said so. He told us to pray to "Our Father in haven." Then she said these precious words over once more. She couldn't say any more of the prayer. This was enough. What comfort that poor sorrowing child, and her widowed mother found in the thought that they had a Father in heaven who couldn't be drowned—who never would die;—a dear kind relative who never could be taken away from them. And as Lilly fell asleep that night, these sweet words were lingering on her lips—"Our Father who art in heaven."

The people of Christ are "blessed above all people," *in their relations.*

The fourth thing in which they are blessed above all people is—in their RICHES.

It is said of Jesus, our Saviour, that "though He was rich"—before he came into this world, "yet for our sakes He became poor, that we," His people, "through His poverty might be rich." Jesus came into this world on purpose to make his people rich. He says, in one place in the New Testament, that He will give His people—"gold, fine gold, gold tried in the fire, that they may be rich." Rev. iii. 18. But it is not the gold and silver of this world that Jesus promises to give his people. It is the gold and silver of heaven that Jesus makes His people rich with. This heavenly gold and silver means the grace and blessing of God. Those who have this kind of riches are blessed above all people for two reasons; one is *their riches can always make them happy; the other is they will last forever.*

The people of Christ are blessed above all people *in having riches that can always make them happy.* The riches that people get in this world cannot make them happy. When Stephen Girard was alive he was the richest man in this city. But you may judge how happy he was, from what he wrote to a friend one day.

"As for myself," said he, "I live like a slave. I am constantly occupied through the day, and often pass the whole night without being able to sleep. I am worn out with the care of my property. If I can only keep busy all day, and sleep all night, this is my highest happiness." Certainly *that* was a very poor kind of happiness.

How often we hear a person say—"Oh, I wish I was rich! If I were only rich I should be so happy!" This is a great mistake. The richest person in the world now, it is said, is Mr. Rothschild, the great Jewish banker of London. All the kings in Europe borrow money from him. One day a person said to him, "You must be a happy man, Mr. Rothschild?"

"Happy!" said he—"I happy! why, the other day, when I was sitting down to dinner, I received a note from some person telling me that if I didn't lend him five hundred pounds he would blow my brains out. And I am afraid to go to sleep at night without having loaded pistols under my pillow. How can I be happy under these circumstances?"

Here you see from *two* of the richest men that ever lived, that the riches of this world, and happiness do not go together.

Now let me show you one who had none of the riches of this world, but whom Jesus had made rich with his grace or blessing, and *that* made him happy.

One windy afternoon, a gentleman went with a friend to visit the alms-house, in his neighborhood. There, sitting before a little fire, was a very aged man. He was almost deaf. His clothes were very poor, and he was so afflicted with the palsy, that his limbs were shaking all the time, and one of his wooden shoes kept a constant pattering on the brick floor. But poor, and deaf, and sick, and almost helpless as he was, it turned out that he was happy.

"What are you doing, Wisby?" said the gentleman to him in a loud voice.

"I am waiting, Sir," was the reply.

"And what are you waiting for?"

"I am waiting for the appearing of my Lord and Saviour," said he.

"And what makes you wish for His appearing?" asked the gentleman.

"Because," said he, "I expect great riches then."

To see if he understood what he was speaking about, the gentleman said,

"What do you expect then, Wisby, and why do you expect it?" The old man, by degrees put on his spectacles, and opening the big Bible on the table near him, and turning to 2 Tim. iv. 7, 8—he read:—"The time of my departure is at hand. I have fought a good fight, I have finished my course, I have kept the faith; henceforth there is laid up for me a crown of righteousness which the Lord, the righteous Judge will give me at that day; and not to me only, but *unto all them also that love His appearing.*"

Here was an old man with none of the riches of this world;—poor, and deaf,—shaken with the palsy, with no home of his own, living in an alms-house, and yet made entirely happy by the riches which Jesus gives. The people of Christ are blessed above all people in having riches that can always make them happy.

And they are blessed above all people, too, *in having riches that will last forever.*

A man may be rich in the things of this world to-day, and poor to-morrow. The Bible says "riches take to themselves wings and flee away." This is like comparing riches to a flock of birds, which light on a man's farm to-day, and to-morrow they are gone.

When I see a spider it often reminds me of rich men. Look at that spider! Solomon says, "The spider taketh hold with her hands, and is in kings' palaces." How carnestly she works in spinning her web; How nimbly she flies up and down! How straight she makes all her lines! How exact, and true all her angles are! What a curious piece of work she makes! How it glitters and shines like silver, as the sunbeams fall upon it! What pains she takes with it! How curiously she spins it out of her own body, and uses up her very life in making it! When it is done, she stretches out one line here, and another there, to make it as secure as possible. And we can fancy this spider talking to herself, and saying,—"Well, now I've got a very snug comfortable home. Here I can catch as many flies as I want, and have a jolly time in eating them. I can stay here, and enjoy myself as long as I live." But just as she is saying this to herself, along comes the chamber-maid. With one stroke of her broom, she sweeps that web all away.

And it is just so with the men who spend their time in gaining the riches of this world. They wear out their very lives in getting them, and then they have no more power to keep them, than the spider has to protect her web from being swept away. They are like the rich man that Jesus spoke about when he was on earth. He said he would pull down his barns and build greater ones, and then he could stow away his goods, and say to himself, now I've got everything that I want. I'll take my ease—I'll eat and drink, and be merry. But that very night death came, and took him away from all his goods. And so it always is with the riches of this world. We never can be sure of them while we live. And when we die we must leave them all behind. When Stephen Girard was living he had many millions of dollars. But when he died he could not take a dollar away with him. He was no better off then than a beggar.

But the riches which Jesus gives to his people are *laid up for them in heaven.* There they are perfectly safe, there they will last forever. If our riches are in this world death will take us away *from* them. If our riches are in heaven, death will take us away *to* them.

A rich man who was not a Christian was lying on his death-bed. He told his servants to bring him his bags of money. He took a bag of gold and clasped it to his heart. Presently, he said :—" Take them away. It won't do! It won't do! I must leave them." And so he died.

Now see a different case. A Christian lady in England had been very well off. But by some means or other, she lost all her property. She was obliged at last to go into the poor-house. She was old and near her end. One day, while a friend was by her side talking to her, he saw her smile, and look very happy. He asked her what she was thinking about that seemed so pleasant : —" Oh!" she said, "I was just thinking what a blessed change it will be when I go from *the poor-house to heaven.* My earthly riches are all gone, but my heavenly riches are all safe. Nobody can take them away from me. They will last forever."

The people of Christ are blessed above all people in their riches, because they can always make them happy, and, because they will last forever.

We have spoken of four things in which Christians are "blessed above all people." The first is *in their names*;—the second is *in their dress*;—the third is *in their relations*;—the fourth is *in their riches.*

Let me entreat you to pray earnestly to Jesus to make you His children, and then indeed you will be "blessed above all people."

VI.

The Blessedness of being a Christian.

"Thou shalt be blessed above all people." DEUT. vii. 14.

VI.

Thou shalt be blessed above all people.' DEUT. vii. 14.

SOMETIMES we see a jewel, or precious stone, that has been very carefully polished, and has a great number of sides, or faces. The upper side of it has a large flat surface. The under side will perhaps rise to a point. Now there will be, perhaps, ten or a dozen different sides or faces. It is a very interesting thing, to take a large jewel of this kind, and examine it carefully. You look into it, or look through it, first from the front. Then you turn it over, and look at one after another of its different sides. They are all beautiful, but each one seems to present some new beauty. As the light falls first on one side and then on another, the shades of color are changing all the time, and the more you look, the more you feel inclined to look. It seems as if it were really growing more beautiful all the time. And a good many texts of scripture are just like such a jewel. They seem to have a great many sides. There are ever so many points from which you can look at them, and they present a different appearance from each. Here, for instance, is the one we are now speaking about. This is like a many-sided jewel. We looked at four of its sides in our last sermon. We are going to look at *four* more of them now. In talking about the *blessedness of being Christians*, last month, we said that they are blessed above all people in *their names:—their dress:—their relations:*—and *their riches.* And when we have had four reasons for anything, the next reason will be number what? Five. Yes. Well then, the *fifth* way in which Christians are blessed above all people is in *their* JOYS.

It is a very common thing, when we are speaking about the joy, or pleasure that persons have, to compare it to a spring, or fountain, from which they drink. And when we thus compare it, we may as well say that the fountain of the Christian's joy is better than any other fountain. Suppose that two fountains were offered us from which to draw all the water that we are to drink. And suppose that one of these fountains was on a beautiful Swiss mountain, supplied by the everlasting ice and snow upon the top of the mountain, and the other far down on a sandy plain. The lower fountain is muddy, and the water in it thick and dirty. It often gets choked up with decaying leaves, and poisonous substances. And then, when the hot summer weather comes, it dries up altogether, so that at the very time the water is most needed there is none in it.

The joy which worldly people have is just like such a fountain on a sandy plain. But the joy which a Christian has is like a spring on a snow-capped mountain. The water which flows from it is pure water. It gushes out clear, cold, and sparkling. And it is flowing out all the time. The heat of summer has no effect upon it. It never stops running.

Some time ago a lady who was traveling, stopped for a few days, at a little village among the beautiful mountains in Wales. The people in that village had to bring all their water from a well, in the middle of the village. Not a single house had a pump belonging to it. At all hours of the day, but especially before breakfast and supper, the people of the village, both old and young, might be seen, passing backwards and forwards with every kind of pitcher kettle, and can, along the lane that led to the well.

One day this lady met a little girl returning from the well with a pail of water in her hand. She said to her,—

"I see a great many people going to that well for water, my little girl, does the well ever run dry?"

"O, yes, ma'am; very often in hot weather."

THE SPRING IN THE MOUNTAIN.

Bible Blessings. p. 159.

"And where do you go for water then?"

"We go to the spring a little way out of town."

"But what do you do if that dries up?"

"Then we go to the spring far up on the side of the mountain:—that is the best water of all."

"And what do you do if that dries up?"

"O, ma'am, that spring is the same winter and summer. *It never dries up!*"

The lady went up to see this spring. She found the water there gushing out from under a great rock. Then it glided away in a clear, sparkling rivulet, not with a torrent leap, and a wild dash, but with a steady flow, and a soft, sweet, gentle murmur. It flowed down the side of the mountain. It was within the reach of every child's little pitcher. There was enough of it to fill all the empty vessels brought to it. The little birds came down there to drink. The sheep and the lambs had trodden down a smooth path for themselves to the brink of the stream; and all the people in the village depended upon that spring when their other supplies failed. And as she stood there looking at it, she said to herself—" Ah! this spring is like the joy that Jesus gives to His people. It is better than all other joys. The joys we find in other things, are like yonder well, down in the village, that dries up in warm weather. But the joy that Jesus gives is like this mountain spring. Its water is clearer, and cooler, and fresher than any other, and it is *a spring that never dries up.*"

Not long ago a lady, who was a Bible visitor in London, was going through her district, which was in one of the poorest parts of that great city. Among other places that she called at, one day, was the home of a poor widow woman, who was a Christian, but just as poor as she could be. She lived in a back kitchen, which had once been used as a wash house. The pavement of the back yard came nearly to the top of the little window, the only one in the room, and shut out almost all the light from it. The room was so dark, that when the lady entered, she could see nothing but a little speck of fire in one cor ner of the room. When her eye got a little accustomed to the darkness she looked round, and saw the room was so damp that the moisture was standing in drops, or trickling in crooked lines down the walls. The only bedstead, in the little cluttered-up room, filled it so that the lady could hardly turn round, or find a place to sit down in. The poor woman who lived there was bent up with rheumatism, and had such a bad cough that she could hardly get a chance to speak to the kind friend who had come to see her.

When the lady asked her how she was, she said, " Thank you, Mrs. Jones, for coming to see me. I have just been praying God to send some good friend to me. I am pretty well, thank you, for me. The cough troubles me some, and so does the rheumatism. But I have still a little fire left from yesterday. I had a penny this morning to get a few tea leaves with, and that seems to ease my cough some. And Sally "—meaning her little girl about nine years old—"is helping to nurse a baby, and her mistress likes her so much that she has taken her into her house altogether; and Johnny"—a little boy, a year younger than Sally—"is gone to a grocer's to run errands, and they have heard of my situation, and give him his meals. So you see, God is very good to me, and I feel that I am *leaping from joy to joy.*"

Ah! if that poor woman had known no joy but such as the world can give, in this time of her trial from poverty, and pain, her joy would have been like the well in the villages that dried up in the hot weather. But she had the joy which Jesus gives and *this* is like the good spring of the mountain —*a spring that never dries up.*

I remember once reading about a spring of fresh water that was found, far out at sea. That spring was so full and so strong, as it came out of the ground, at the bottom of the sea, that it could send a stream of fresh water rising up through all the depths of the briny ocean, and pouring itself out in freshness on the surface. And the joy which Jesus gives is just like such a spring. Its pure water can rise up even through a sea of troubles like those in which this poor woman was plunged. and make her happy in the very midst of those troubles.

The fifth thing in which the Christian is blessed above all people is in *his joy.*

The sixth thing in which he is so blessed is in HIS HONOR.

Men think a great deal of honor. They will make any effort and run any risk, and face any danger in order to gain it. And yet there is no honor in the world, like that which Jesus gives his people. The Bible calls it the "*honor which cometh from God.*"

In countries like England, where a king or queen is the head of the nation, it is considered the highest honor to be near the monarch and to be permitted to do any thing for him.

Now, suppose, that you and I were living

in London. And suppose that we were jewellers by trade, and had a large store on Oxford Street, in the fashionable part of London. And suppose that one day Queen Victoria should come into our store, or shop as they call it in England. She buys the most splendid set of jewels that we have, and tells us that she intends hereafter to buy all her jewels from us; and that when she wants any gold or silver things she will send to us to make them for her. How much honored we should feel! How soon we should get a new sign, and have painted on it, in big round letters—

NEWTON & CO.,

JEWELERS TO HER MAJESTY.

What a rush we should have to our store of the nobility of England, and how rich we should get in a little while! We should feel it a great honor to make jewels for the king or queen. But Jesus is the king of his people. He is the king of heaven. The Bible calls Him "The Great King;"—"the King of Kings." O, there is no king like Jesus, and no honor like that of working for Him! But when we become Christians, Jesus engages us to be His servants, and to work for Him. One reason why I so much love to preach is that in doing it, I feel I am *preaching for Jesus.* All that a Christian does, he does for Jesus, and all that he suffers, he suffers for Jesus. If we are real Christians, we are working for Jesus now, and when we die we shall be brought very near to Jesus. We shall be even nearer than the angels are. Jesus never became an angel, but He did once become a man. He has not got an angel's nature now, but He has got a man's nature. He has the same nature that you and I have. He is not the brother of the angels, but He is *our* brother. He is bone of our bone, and flesh of our flesh. We are His *nearest* relatives. We shall stand the closest to Him in heaven, of all His creature . How wonderful this is! What an honor we have here! Yes, and not only shall we be brought near to this King, but He will make *us kings ourselves!* Jesus will make all His people kings, and give them all crowns which they shall wear forever.

There was a nobleman in Scotland, known as the Duke of Hamilton. This Duke had two sons. It is the law in Scotland, that when a man dies, who is a nobleman, a duke or a lord, his oldest son takes his name or title, and becomes duke, or lord, after him; and also takes his property. But if the oldest son dies before his father, then the next son takes his place, and his title, and his property. The oldest son of the Duke of Hamilton, of whom I am now speaking, was a very pious youth, but he fell into the consumption, and died, before he became of age. One day, a short time before his death, the minister of the church to which the family belonged, came to see him. He prayed with him, and after prayer, the youth took his Bible from under his pillow, and turning to 2 Tim. iv. 7, he read these words:—" I have fought a good fight. I have finished my course. I have kept the faith; henceforth there is laid up for me *a crown of righteousness.*" Turning to his father, who stood by, he said—"Father, this is all my comfort." Then calling his younger brother to him, who was to take the title and property, after his father's death, he spoke very affectionately to him, and ended with these words—"And now, Douglas, in a little while you shall be a duke, and *I shall be a king.*" What honor can the earth give like this! The Christian is blessed above all people in *his honor.*

The seventh thing in which the Christian is thus blessed above all others, is in HIS CARE.

I mean by this the care which God takes of him. What a wonderful thing it is that the great God, who sitteth in the heavens, and governs all things, should stoop so low as to take care of poor, sinful creatures like you and me! And yet he does so. If I take a jewel, or precious stone, and shut it up in my hand, and hold it tight, how safe it is, just so long as I hold it so. And yet the Bible tells us that this is the very way in which God holds his people. They are kept "in the hollow of His hand" all the time. He watches over them night and day. He puts his everlasting arms underneath them. He spreads His everlasting wings over them. When Satan wants to injure them, God won't let him, and he can't do anything till God gives him leave. We read in the Bible about how Satan tried to injure Job. He thought, if he could only get at him, and destroy his property, and kill his children, and take away his health, then Job would give up his trust in God, and become a wicked man. God wouldn't let him do this at first. But at last He told him he might do it. And as soon as he got permission he did it, pretty quickly. In a little while poor Job was stripped of his property, his family and his health. He lay in the ashes covered with boils from head to foot. Now if we could have seen Job in the midst of all this poverty, suffering, and sorrow, we should, perhaps, have been tempted to think that God had forgotten him, and wasn't taking care of him at all. But He was. He was never taking better care of him than when He let Satan bring all this trouble upon him. God made it "all work together for good" to Job, as he has promised to do, in the Bible, for all His people. These troubles didn't make Job give up his religion, as Satan said they would. On the contrary, he clung to it closer than ever. In the midst of all his trials he looked up to God and said, "Though He slay me, yet will I trust in Him." And then God delivered him from his troubles. He healed his boils, and made him well. He gave him as many children as he had before, and twice as much property. So that the thing by which Satan thought he was going to ruin Job, was the very thing which God used to make him a better, and a richer, and a happier man than ever he was before. Job had reason to feel very much obliged to

Satan for bringing all that trouble upon him. It was the best thing that ever happened to him.

And it was just the same with Joseph. His brethren thought they would be sure to prevent his dreams from being fulfilled, by taking him away from his father, and selling him as a slave into Egypt. But God took such care of Joseph that He made *that* the very means of bringing his dreams to pass. No doubt Joseph thought it was very hard, when he was lowered down into that pit, and when he was kept so long in prison in Egypt. And yet these were the best things that ever happened to him. God took such care of him that He made all these things work for good to Joseph. And so He did for Daniel, when his enemies cast him into the lion's den. And so He did for Shadrack, Mesheck and Abednego, when the king threw them into the burning fiery furnace. And so He does for His people always. God takes such care of every Christian that nothing can ever happen to him that is not *all for the best.*

There is a beautiful illustration of this, in an eastern story told of a pious Jew. His name was Rabbi Akibo. He had been persecuted by the enemies of his religion, and driven away from his home. He was obliged to travel about the country, from place to place, so as to keep out of the way of his enemies. In his journeys, he used to carry with him a lamp, which he could light at night to read the Bible, which was his constant study. He also carried with him, a chicken cock, or rooster, to wake him up early in the morning, by crowing, and a donkey, or jack-ass, on which he rode.

One day he had been travelling all day, and felt pretty tired. When it came towards sunset, he began to look round for a place to rest in for the night. Presently he saw before him a nice looking village, and drove up to it, thinking, no doubt, that he would soon find an inn, or some friendly house that would give him a night's lodging. But in this he was mistaken. There was no inn, in the village, and none of the villagers would give him shelter in their houses. He was, therefore, obliged to drive through the village and look for the best resting place he could find in the first woods that he came to. Then he sought out a sheltered spot, under a thick tree, and as he sat down upon the grass, he said to himself, "It's very hard not to have a house to shelter one from the cold night air, but God is good, it's all for the best."

Then he seated himself under the tree, and lighted his lamp, and thought he would have a pleasant time in studying his Bible. But before he had read many verses, a storm arose. The wind blew out his lamp, and the rain prevented him from lighting it again. "What a pity," said he, "that I can't even enjoy the pleasure of reading my precious Bible! But God is good, and its all for the best."

Then he covered himself up, and lay down upon the grass to got a few hour's sleep. He had hardly closed his eyes, however, before a wolf came by, and seized the rooster from the low branch of a tree on which it was resting, and quietly made a meal of it.

"I'm very sorry for this new loss," said poor Rabbi; "my watchful companion is gone. Now I have none to wake me in the mornings to study my Bible. But God is good, and it's all for the best."

He had scarcely finished these words, before he was alarmed by the roar of a lion. The next moment the savage beast sprang upon his trusty donkey, and devoured it.

This was the heaviest blow of all. "What shall I do now?" exclaimed the poor traveler. "My lamp is gone. My rooster is gone. My poor donkey too, is gone. Everything is gone. But God is good; it's all for the best.

After all this, he passed, of course, a troubled night. He had very little sleep. Early in the morning he went back to the village to see if he could buy a horse, or another donkey, to carry him and his things, as he went on his journey. But what was his surprise, on entering the village, to find not a single person there alive.

It seems that during the night a band of robbers had entered the village, murdered all the inhabitants, and robbed their houses of all the valuable things found in them. You can imagine how great was the surprise of the pious Rabbi, at the wonderful care God had taken of him. As soon as he had recovered a little from his surprise, he lifted up his voice, and said:

"O, God, Thou God of Abraham, Isaac, and Jacob, how wonderful Thou art! Now I see how blind and ignorant, we poor mortals are, when we look upon those things as evils which are meant for our good. Thou only art wise, and kind, and merciful. If those hard-hearted people had not driven me away from their village, I should have perished with them. If the storm had not put out my lamp, its light would have drawn the robbers to my resting-place, and I should have been killed. And if the wild beasts had not devoured my two companions, the crowing of the cock, or the braying of the ass, would have told the robbers of my presence, and they would have murdered me. Praised be Thy name forever. Thou art good and all that happens is for the best."

Christians are blessed above all people in the care that is taken of them; or *in their care.*

The last thing that I shall speak of as that in which Christians are blessed above all people is in THEIR TREASURES.

Our treasures are what we love the most, or what we set our hearts on. Jesus said to His people when He was on earth, "where your treasure is *there* will your heart be also." People of the world have their treasures here on the earth. Christian people have their treasures laid up in heaven. One man's treasure is the splendid house which he has built. And perhaps as soon as it is finished, it catches fire, and is burned down. Another man's treasure is his wife, or child. But how soon sickness may seize on these, and death may carry them away. Another man's treasure is some high office. He sets his heart on gaining that office. He tries very hard and long to gain it. He gains it at last, but he finds it is not what he expected it to be. It doesn't make him happy.

I remember hearing of a little boy, once, who saw a bird's nest, in the top of a high tree, on the edge of a woods, near the road along which he played every day on his way to school. He often stopped to look up at it. He thought of the pretty blue eggs in it beautifully speckled all over. He wished he could get the nest. If he only had it, he would take a pin and make a little hole at each end of the eggs, and blow the contents out, and then string them like beads on a thread, and hang them up in his room by the side of his bed. They would look so pretty there. The more he thought of it, the more he wanted to have it. He set his heart on getting that nest. He thought it would be such a treasure. Sometimes when he stopped to look at the tree and saw how high the nest was, and how slender the branches of the tree were near it, he thought he might fall, in trying to get it, and break his limbs, or his neck, and then he almost gave it up. But again when he got thinking about the pretty eggs in it he felt as if he must have that nest.

At last, one Saturday afternoon, he made up his mind that he would go to the tree by himself, and try to secure the treasure on which his heart was set. So he went. When he came to the tree he buttoned up his jacket, and put off his shoes, so that he might cling to the tree better with his feet. And then he began to climb up the tree. At first he got on pretty well, for the branches were low, and rather close together. After a while it became much harder. Still he kept on. He tore his clothes. He scratched his hands and his face. The branches began to bend under him, yet he wouldn't give it up. Higher and higher he went. At last he seized the treasure which he had longed for so much. He looked eagerly into the nest, but there were *no eggs in it!* It was empty. He had run all that risk, and taken all that trouble for nothing.

How many of the treasures which the people of this world try to get, are just like this empty bird-nest! But it is very different with the Christian's treasures. These never disappoint those who gain them. However much we may think and talk about them, and long to have them, they will be a thousand times better than all our thoughts or expectations.

Not long ago a young lady called at the house of her minister. When she entered the parlor, she found his two little boys, Arthur and Willie, seated on the floor, surrounded by beautiful toys and pictures, which had been sent them as presents, and with which they seemed highly pleased. There was a dissected map, a magic lantern, a humming top, and other pretty and amusing things. The young lady was much pleased with what she saw, and said, "Why, boys, are all these your treasures?"

Arthur, who was about eight years old, said, "No, ma'am, these are not our treasures. These are only our *playthings*—our treasures are not here."

"Where are they?" asked the lady.

"They are in heaven," said the little boy.

"And what treasures have you in heaven?" she asked.

"We have a harp and a crown," said Arthur. This was the right feeling to have. And this is just the feeling that true Christians have. They are bright and happy, as those boys were. They enjoy the good things that God gives them, the money and the property they have here, as those boys enjoyed their presents. But then, like those boys, they feel that these are only their playthings, not their treasures. Their treasures are the harp and crown which Jesus has prepared for them in heaven. These are the treasures on which their hearts are set. They are worth more than anybody can tell. The crown which the Queen of England wears is very beautiful, and very valuable. But it is very easy to tell just how much it is worth. We could weigh it, and find out how many ounces of gold are in it. We know how much gold is worth an ounce, and so we could tell the value of the gold in that crown. Then we could find out the value of the jewels that are in it, and so, by adding these together, we could tell exactly what *that* crown is worth. But nobody can tell how much the crown is worth that Jesus is preparing for you and me, if we really love Him. All the gold, and the silver, and the jewels in the world, *a thousand times over* could not buy it. O, there is no treasure like this. Christians are blessed above all people in *their treasure.*

We have mentioned four things in this sermon, in which Christians are blessed above all people. These are—their joys, their honor, their care, their treasure. And, taking both sermons together, there are *eight* things in which Christians are more blessed than others, viz :—in *their names*, *their dress*, *their relations*, *their riches*, *their joy*, *their honor*, *their care*, and *their treasure.*

Now you can talk about this blessedness, and tell what is consists of, but if you want to be able to *feel* it, as well as talk about it; if you want to have it for your own, you must pray earnestly to Jesus to change your hearts, and make you His loving children. Then you will know what a blessed thing it is to be a Christian, not because you have heard a sermon on the subject, but because you feel it in your hearts.

Lord Jesus Christ! make us all thy dear children, that we may be blessed above all people in our names, in our dress, in our relations, in our riches, in our joy, in our honor, in our care and in our treasures, and we will give Thee all the praise and the glory forever.—*Amen.*

VII.

Troubles turned to Blessings.

"Blessed is the man whom Thou chastenest."

PSALM xciv. 12.

VII.

"Blessed is the man whom Thou chastenest."
PSALM xciv. 12.

"CHASTENEST" is a hard word. Let us see what it means before we go any further. The meaning is the same as that of the word chastise. Suppose that two boys, from your school, play truant one day. Your teacher hears of it. He says—"Never mind; when they come back to school, I'll chastise them." What would he mean by that? He would mean that he intended to punish them. It would be right for the teacher to punish those boys. And the reason why he would do it, would be, not because it was any pleasure to him to hear them cry, and see them suffering pain, but because he wished to keep them from doing wrong. When he took those boys, each in turn by the hand, and took his rod to whip them, he was teaching them. And if he succeeded in making them feel that it was wrong to play truant, and if the boys made up their minds never to play truant again, then that chastisement or punishment, was a blessing to them. And whatever teaches us a lesson that does us good is a blessing. It was a heavy trial, a severe chastisement to old Jacob when God took away Joseph from him. But God saw that he was loving Joseph too much. He saw that unless he stopped loving him so much it would do him a great deal of harm. So he took Joseph away. It almost broke Jacob's heart. But it taught him to love God more, and to love Joseph less, and in this way chastening or trial was a blessing to him.

And so, when David said, "Blessed is the man whom thou chastenest" he meant to say that when God sends any trouble, or trial, or affliction on a Christian, He always intends it to do him good, or prove a blessing to him, in one way, or another. If sickness comes upon him it comes to bless him. If he loves his property God makes the loss a blessing. If his parents, or relations, or friends die, some may be ready to say —" O what a dreadful evil that is!"—but God turns even *that* into a blessing. " Blessed is the man whom Thou chastenest." Now since this is the case what a happy thing it is to be a Christian!

I dare say a good many of you have heard of a certain stone, that used to be talked about a great deal, called " the philosopher's stone." Very learned men, who are not always very wise men, used to suppose that there was such a stone, and that it had the power of turning everything it touched to gold. Now just let us suppose that there was such a great stone, and that you and I had found it. What a grand time we would have! When we were short of money we could get a lot of pebble stones, and touch them with this wonderful stone, and lo! they would all be lumps of gold. We could drop it into a pail of water, and we should have that pail full of melted gold. We could go into our mother's china closet, and touch the cups and saucers, the plates and dishes, and in an instant they would all be turned to gold. We shoudn't care about the mines of California, or the oil wells of Pennsylvania, for we should have as much gold as we wanted without any trouble.

But the words of David, in our text, show us that a true Christian is better off than the man would be who had the philosopher's stone, and could turn everything to gold. The Christian has something which turns everything to *good.* This is better than gold. Too much gold is one of the worst things we can have. It has ruined many people both in body and soul. And it might ruin us if we had it. It is a great deal better to have everything that touches us, or happens to us, turn to *good*, than turn to gold. And if we are Christians, this will be so with us. Even the chastenings, that is, the sorrows, or trials, or afflictions that happen to us will turn to blessings. For God has promised to "make *all things work together for good* to those who love Him." Romans, viii. 20.

You know there are offices, down town, called Insurance Offices. Some of these are called "Fire Insurance Offices." They insure buildings against loss from fire. Suppose this church should take fire some night, and burn down. That would be a great loss to us It would be a loss from fire. But this church is insured. . The wardens of the church have been to one of those offices, and paid them some money to insure the church against loss from fire. This doesn't mean that the people in that office will prevent this church from being burnt. But it *does* mean that if it ever should be burnt, they will pay us money enough to build it up again, just as it was before the fire.

Some of those offices are for *insuring lives.* A man pays a certain sum of money in one of these offices to insure his life. This doesn't mean that they can prevent him from getting sick or dying; but it does mean that if he should die they will pay money to his family to help in supporting them. And this is called a *life insurance.*

And then some of these offices are for what are called *Marine Insurances.* This means that they insure property against loss from the dangers of the sea. For instance, suppose that you and I were merchants down on the wharf. We are going to send a vessel loaded with flour to Rio Janeiro, in South America. That vessel will have many dangers to meet. She may spring a leak, and sink at sea. Or she may be wrecked by storms, and never reach port. Then all our property would be lost. So we insure the vessel and her cargo. We pay a certain amount of money to one of those offices, and they insure the vessel and her cargo. This doesn't mean that they will prevent any storm from overtaking our vessel, or that they will keep her from being wrecked. But it does mean that in case she should be wrecked, they will pay us as much money as the vessel and her cargo were worth. And so we feel safe about our vessel because she is insured.

Now something like this takes place when we become Christians. Our blessed Saviour may be said to keep *a general insurance office.* He insures the souls of His people against all harm. He does not engage to keep His people from ever being sick, or ever having any sorrow or trouble. But whenever sickness or sorrow comes upon them, He engages to make it all work for good to them. He will turn it all into blessing. And this is what David means when he says—"Blessed is the man whom thou chastenest."

Everything about a Christian is insured. Nobody can do him any harm. Jesus will turn every trial that comes upon him into a blessing.

I wish to speak of *three* ways in which Jesus makes trouble or chastisement a blessing to His people.

The first way in which Jesus makes trouble

a blessing to His people, is, by SAVING THEM FROM DANGER BY IT.

One reason why we find it so hard to believe, when trouble comes upon us, that God intends it to do us good, and be a blessing, is that we can't see *how* it is to be so. We almost always have to wait awhile, before this can be seen. But as soon as we find out what God intends any trial to do for us, we see that it *was* a real blessing.

A merchant was one day returning from market on horse-back. His saddle-bags were filled with money which had got for what he had been selling. Soon after he started, it began to rain. It rained very hard, and he soon got wet through. This vexed him very much, and he went on murmuring to himself that God had sent him such bad weather for his journey. Pretty soon he reached the border of a thick piece of woods. Just as he was going into the woods, he was very much alarmed to see a robber standing by the side of the road with a gun in his hand. As soon as he came up to him, the robber levelled

THE ROBBER.

his gun, took aim, and pulled the trigger,—but it didn't go off. The same rain which had wet him through had made the robber's powder so damp that it wouldn't fire. And before he could prime his gun again, the merchant had put spurs to his horse, and escaped. As soon as he found that he was safe, he said to himself, "How wrong it was for me to murmur against the rain. I thought it was a great trouble to have it. But now I see God sent it to be a blessing. If it had not been for that rain, I should have lost my life and property."

When Mary, commonly known as "bloody Mary," was Queen of England, a great many of the good Protestant ministers, and people, were persecuted because they would not give up their religion. Among these, there was a very earnest, faithful minister, whose name was Gilpin. He was so fully convinced of the truth of what the Bible teaches us, on the subject of which we are now speaking, that he was in the habit of saying, of everything that happened to him,

"It's all for the best." Well, one time, he received a summons to go to London, and be tried for his life, before those who were putting the Protestants to death. On the journey, he fell, and broke his leg.

"Do you think *this* is all for the best?" said somebody to him.

"I've no doubt of it," said he. Of course he couldn't travel with a broken leg. He had to wait on the road, till his leg got well. In the meantime, Queen Mary died. Her sister, Elizabeth, became the Queen of England, and the persecution of the Protestants ceased. When Mr. Gilpin got well, he went home again in peace. And thus we see how truly his broken leg was a blessing to him, in saving his life.

Some years ago, an American man-of-war was lying at anchor, in the Bay of Naples. The commander of that ship, was the Commodore of the fleet, then in the Mediterranean Sea. The Commodore had his son with him on board. He was a little fellow, of eight or nine years old; a very bright, smart boy, and a great pet with all the officers and crew. He was very fond of climbing up the rigging, and would sometimes venture farther than it was safe for him to go. One day, while his father was in the cabin, taking a nap, after dinner, he was playing on deck. No one seemed to be noticing him, and he thought he would go up the rigging of the main-mast, and see how far he could climb. He got up to the cross-trees. Then he went to the top gallant-mast; and then to the royal yards. That was the highest yard, or cross-piece, belonging to the main-mast. There he rested awhile. Then he swarmed up the mast, and got on to what the sailors call "the main-truck." This is the circular piece of wood that is at the very top of the mast. How he did it, I cannot imagine; but by some means, or other, he managed to get up, and stand erect, on that little piece of wood, at that giddy, dangerous height. He enjoyed his lofty position for awhile. But when he thought of getting down, he began to feel troubled. And now the officers and sailors on deck, saw him, and were greatly distressed. They trembled to think of the danger their favorite was in. They ran about the deck in great excitement. No one knew what to do. If he stooped to get down, he would be sure to fall. If they attempted to go to him, their weight would sway the trembling mast, and shake him off, and he would be dashed to pieces. In the midst of this excitement, the Commodore came on deck. He saw at a glance, the peril of his darling boy. He knew there was but one thing to save him. He rushed into the cabin and seized a loaded gun in one hand, and a speaking trumpet in the other. The little fellow was trembling, and losing his presence of mind. Every one feared each moment to see his mangled body fall to the deck. But now the Commodore has returned. He stands on the quarter-deck. He lifts the speaking trumpet to his mouth, and in a clear, ringing voice, cries out—"*Jump into the water, or I'll shoot you!*" The little fellow stoops down to gather up his strength. He gives a spring, out into the air, to clear the deck of the ship, and then like an arrow, he goes diving down into the calm, clear water of the Bay. As quick as lightning, a dozen or twenty sailors plunge in after him. Soon he is safe on deck, and the tears flow down his father's weather-beaten cheeks like rain, as he presses his dear boy to his bosom, snatched from such a dreadful death.

It seemed like a cruel thing in that father, to threaten to shoot his boy. But it wasn't so. It was *the kindest thing he ever did for him.* It saved him from a terrible death. Nothing but that jump could have saved him. His father knew this, when he drove him to it. And so God often sends trouble, to drive His people away from things that will harm them. The first way in which He makes trouble a blessing to His people, is *by saving them from danger.*

The second way in which He does this is BY FITTING THEM FOR USEFULNESS.

Hardly anything can be made useful without trouble. Suppose you had a great lump of golden ore, from one of the mines in California. Well, you examine it, and see that there are pieces of gold here and there in it, which make it very valuable. But they are all mixed up with earth and rocks, in such a way that nothing can be done with it. Before you can make any use of it, you must break it into pieces and put it in the furnace, and raise a great fire over it, till the gold melts, and runs out from the dross. Then you get the pure gold by itself, and can employ it for any useful purpose that you wish.

There is a sheaf of grain from the harvest field. It is very valuable, but in its present state it can't be used for any good purpose. It must be thrashed to separate it from the ear. Then it must be fanned, or winnowed, to separate it from the chaff. And then it must be taken to the mill, and ground into flour, before it is fit for use.

And Christians are like gold in the ore.

The good in them is mixed up with dross. God has to use the hammer, and the fire of trouble, or affliction upon them, to melt the gold in them, and separate it from the dross.

Christians are like the grain in the ear. God has to thrash them, and winnow them, and grind them, before they are fit for the purpose for which He wants to use them. And He makes use of trouble to do this.

Many of you have read Bunyan's Pilgrim Progress. That is one of the most useful books in the world. Next to the Bible, it has perhaps done more good than any book that was ever printed. John Bunyan, who wrote that book, was a celebrated preacher. He lived at a time when men were persecuted for their religion. Great crowds used to go to hear him preach. This made his enemies very angry. In order to stop him from preaching, they had him put in prison. They kept him there for a number of years. Mr. Bunyan's friends thought this was very strange. They couldn't understand why

God should permit such a useful man to be shut up so long in prison, when he might have done so much good by preaching. They thought his imprisonment was nothing but a trouble to him. But they were mistaken. It was a great blessing, both to him, and to the world. While he was in prison, John Bunyan wrote "The Pilgrim's Progress." He never could have written it if he had not been kept so long in prison. And he has done more good by that book than could have been done by all the sermons he might have preached during the years he was in prison. And it is always so when God sends trouble on His people. He intends to make it a blessing to them by preparing them for usefulness, either in this life, or in the life to come.

I met an interesting story, not long ago,—about Johnny Truman, and his *iron-boot.* This little boy had a disease, called the rickets. It made the bones of his foot and ankle soft, so that they were bending, and growing out of proper shape, as he walked upon them. His mother took him to a physician, to see what had better be done with him. The physician told her to have an iron-boot made, for his foot, and to make him wear it, ever day for a year. So the boot was made and put on. But Johnny found it very awkward, unpleasant, and painful. Think of a stiff iron-boot, on the soft tender foot of a little boy! It never would bend the least bit in the world. There was no spring to it. The muscles wouldn't stretch. The joints wouldn't move. He couldn't run. He couldn't jump. He could only drag it on, as he walked slowly along. Poor Johnny, it was a very hard thing for him. Sometimes the neighbors would say as he was limping along:—

"There goes poor Johnny Truman, with his iron boot. It's real cruel in his mother to make him wear it when he hates it so much."

And sometimes he would come to his mother and say;—

"Oh! mother do take this iron-boot off.

It's so hard to get along with. It almost kills me. I don't care if I am lame. I don't care if my ankle is out of joint. I don't care how I am when I grow up. All I want is *to get this boot off.*" And then Johnny would worry and fret as if his mother had put the boot on just on purpose to give him trouble. Yet it wasn't so. The iron boot was necessary to support the limb till the bones grew strong and healthy. But Johnny had no faith in it. He didn't believe it would do him any good. He said he was sure there was no use in it, and so instead of trusting his mother, and the doctor, he was fretting, and worrying about it, all the time.

A lady, who was staying at the house, got tired of hearing his complaints, and she said to his mother, one day,

"Mrs. Truman, why don't you take the boot off that boy, and let him take the consequences? I'm sure I would."

His mother was grieved. She looked

with tender love upon her little boy, and as she stroked his head, she said :—

"I must do for my child, not what is most pleasant for him now, but what will be most useful for him hereafter. Johnny will thank me, one day, for what I am doing now. If he wouldn't think about it so much, it wouldn't be so hard to bear. He has a great many things to make him comfortable and happy, in spite of his iron-boot, and that won't last long."

Johnny hung down his head. He felt ashamed of himself. He knew how many kind thinks his mother was doing for him all the time, and that even the iron-boot was for his good.

At last the year of painful trial passed away. The disease was removed. The iron-boot was taken off. Johnny grew up to be a tall, handsome young man, with straight, strong limbs and a firm, quick tread. And what do you think he oftenest said to his mother? Many and many a time he would throw his arms round her neck, and say—

"Oh, mother I never can thank you enough for making me wear that iron-boot! *It was the best thing you ever did for me.* If it hadn't been for that I would have a poor cripple all my life."

Thus you see how Johnny's trouble was made a blessing to him. Well, just in the same way every trial that we have, is *an iron-boot* that our heavenly Father puts upon us. Don't let us fret and worry about it; but let us bear it patiently, because we may be sure that God intends it to do us good in some way. The second way in which God makes trouble a blessing to his people is *by fitting them for usefulness.*

The third way in which God makes trouble a blessing to His people is BY LEADING THEM TO TRUE HAPPINESS.

When summer comes, among the Alps, in Switzerland, the shepherds lead their flocks far up the sides of the mountains, where the best pasture can be found. If they stay down on the plains, and in the valleys, the pasture will fail, and they will have nothing to eat. But away up the mountains there is plenty of good pasture. One summer a shepherd was driving his flock up towards those pleasant pastures. But there was one place in the road which he could not get the sheep to go past. There was a narrow chasm, or opening right across the path, and when they came to the edge of it, instead of leaping over, as he wanted them to do, they would turn round, and scamper away, in another direction. He tried several times to get them past that place, but in vain. At last he took up in his arms a little lamb, belonging to one of his sheep. The mother sheep, or dam, watched him closely to see what he was going to do with it. Instead of driving his flock from behind them, he now went on before them, carrying the lamb in his arms. He crossed over the chasm in the path, and went straight on, up the side of the mountain. The mother sheep followed after the shepherd who had her lamb in his arms. She leaped across the opening and kept close to the shepherd. The other sheep followed her, one after another, till, pretty soon, the whole flock were going up the mountain, after the shepherd to the place where the good pastures were to which he desired to lead them.

And God deals with His people in just the same way. He calls to them in His word, and by His ministers to become Christians and walk in the narrow way which will lead them up the heavenly mountain, to the good pastures in which He would have them feed forever. But, like the sheep just spoken of, they turn aside, and wander off in the wrong direction. Then God sends trouble upon them, and takes away their children or other blessings from them till at last, like the sheep whose lamb was taken from her side, they follow Him in the path up which he desires to lead them.

Let me give you another illustration of

the way in which God sometimes turns the troubles of his people into blessings.

A Christian minister was once visiting a large botanical garden. He walked along the paths, looking carefully at one plant after another. Presently he came to a fine large pomegranate bush or tree. On examining it more closely, he found that some of the branches had been taken off, and the principal stem of the tree had been cut almost through. As the gardener was standing near, he said to him:

"Pray, sir, tell me why you have made this deep cut in the stem of this pomegranate?"

"Sir," said the gardener, "this tree used to be very strong and vigorous, but it bore nothing but leaves. I was therefore obliged to prune off some of the branches, and cut the stem in this manner, and when it was almost cut through it began to bear plenty of fruit."

Now, if this tree had been able to think and speak, as you and I can, no doubt it would have thought it very hard in the gardener to cut it so. It would have said that he was cruel, and was doing it a great deal of harm. Yet, when it came to find that the effect of all that cutting was not to injure it, but to do it good, and make it fruitful, it would have seen that instead of being a trouble to it, it was a real blessing when the gardener pruned and cut it so.

And this is just the way God deals with His people. Until we become real Christians we are like trees in His garden, that have leaves on them, but no fruit. And if we don't hear Him when He calls us; if we don't give Him our hearts, and love and serve Him truly, then He is obliged to prune off our branches, and cut us deeply by trials and afflictions. Let me show you how God did this in one case.

A father and mother were blessed with four dear children. They were healthy, happy children, the very joy of their parents' hearts. Those parents were very well off. They had everything about them they could desire of the good things of this world. But they were not Christians. They did not love and serve Jesus. They were in His garden like trees that bore nothing but leaves. When Jesus, the heavenly gardener, came looking for fruit from them, he found none. And so, like a wise and faithful gardener, he was obliged to take the knife, and prune and cut, in order to make them bear fruit. With the first stroke of the knife their youngest child, a bright and promising boy, was cut down. One morning he fell into the fish pond near their house, and was drowned. This was a heavy blow to them. It filled their hearts with sorrow, and spread gloom and sadness through their dwelling. But it didn't have the good effect which the heavenly gardener intended. He was obliged to take up the knife again. The only daughter, a lovely girl of sixteen, was smitten with a fever, and died. This greatly increased their distress and sorrow, but it did not bring them to Jesus He was obliged to use the knife again. Their oldest son, who had come home from college to spend his vacation, was killed by the accidental discharge of a gun while hunting. Now, the poor mother was nearly wild with grief. Her heart was almost broken. The stem was cut well nigh through. And now it began to bear fruit. The sorrowing mother went to church, hoping to find some comfort. There she heard the voice of Jesus, speaking from His word, and saying—"Come unto me, all ye that labor, and are heavy laden, and I will give you rest." She came to Jesus in her sorrow. She found pardon and peace, joy, and happiness in Him. Her husband became a Christian too. And now the trees that had been so severely pruned, and cut, began to bear good fruit. Those afflicted parents found more real pleasure, and enjoyment in serving God than ever they had known before. The good Shepherd had led them up the mountain by a very rough, steep path. But He had brought them to the best pasture. They often say:—"God took away our children in mercy to our souls."

They were great troubles indeed, which God sent upon them, but He had turned them into blessings. He had done so *by leading them to true happiness.*

And thus we have spoken of three ways in which God turns the troubles of His people into blessings. *The first is by saving them from danger. The second is by fitting them for usefulness. The third is by leading them to happiness.*

And if this be so then how important it is that we should become Christians while we are young! Dr. Watts says, in one of his sweet, simple hymns—

> "'Twill save us from a thousand *snares*,
> To mind religion young."

That is very true. But it will save us from a thousand *sorrows* too, as well as snares. If the tree only bears fruit as it ought to do, the gardener is saved the trouble of having to prune it, and cut it. But if it don't bear fruit he must use the knife. And it is just the same with us. If we don't hear God, when He calls us, as Samuel did, we make it necessary for Him to send trouble on us, and break our hearts with sorrow, in order to make us His children and save our souls. But don't let us wait for this. Let us come to Jesus now, as soon as He calls us. Then we shall be saved from *great* trials. And when lesser troubles come upon us, we shall find comfort in the words of David, when he said;—"Blessed is the man whom Thou chastenest." We shall know that every trial sent upon us is intended to do us good. O, it is a happy thing to be a Christian, for every trouble that comes upon us God will turn into a blessing. This is one of the sweetest of "The Bible Blessings," of which we are speaking. May God give it to you all, my dear children, for Jesus' sake! Amen!

VIII.

The Blessedness of Trusting God.

"Whoso trusteth in the Lord, happy is he."

PROVERBS xvi. 20.

VIII.

"Whoso trusteth in the Lord, happy is he."
PROVERBS xvi. 20.

IT is wonderful how much is said in the Bible about trusting God. Here, in the text Solomon says "Whoso trusteth in Him is *happy*." In several places it says that they who trust in Him are *blessed*. It tells us in one place that "they who trust in the Lord shall *not be afraid*." Ps. cxxv. 1. It tells us in another place that "The Lord *delivers* those who trust in Him," Ps. xxii. 4:—that "His *mercy will surround* them," Ps. xxxii. 10:—that "He *knoweth*," or loveth them, Nahum i. 7:—that "He *will keep them* in *perfect peace*," Ps. xxvi. 3:—and that "He will *save* them that trust in Him," Ps. xxxvii. 4. Now the Bible would not say so much about trusting in God unless it was a very important thing.

To learn to trust in God is the most impor tant lesson we ever have to learn. Whei you see a real Christian who is always happy, the secret of his happiness—the thing that makes him so ready to rejoice, and sing all the time is just this—he has learned how to trust God. And when you see a person who never seems happy, but is worrying and fretting continually, and always afraid that something dreadful is going to happen, the simple reason why that person is so unhappy is that he has never learned to trust God. But if we learn to know Jesus, as our Saviour, and to trust Him as the Bible teaches us to do, we never need be unhappy about anything. When the pious patriarch Job had lost all his children and all his property, and his body was covered all over with dreadful boils—he looked up to God and said—"Though He slay me yet will I trust in Him." How well Job had learned this lesson of trusting God! And God by His grace can teach us to learn it as well as Job did. And if we do learn it we shall understand what Solomon means when he says, "Whoso trusteth in the Lord happy is he." Trusting God will teach us how to be happy at all times, and under all circumstances. This is *the great secret of happiness.*

Some years ago there was a poor slave in one of the West India Islands who had become a Christian. He had learned well this lesson of trusting God. The missionary whose church he attended was talking to him one day. "Well Sambo," said the missionary, "if your driver should lay you down and flog you what would you do?" "Me love God and trust Him all de same."

"But if you could get no meat to eat what would you do?"

"Me eat, me tank me Fader: me no eat, me tank me Fader. Me live, me tank me Fader: me die, me tank me Fader."

What a noble answer that was! How much like Job's saying—"Though he slay me yet will I trust in Him." How happy we should be indeed, if we could learn *thus* to put our trust in God! We are not fit to live till we learn to trust in God. Would you be willing to go to sea in a vessel that had no anchor? No. Such a vessel is not fit to go to sea. But trust in God is just as important to us as the anchor is to the ship. Would you be willing to live in a house that was just built on the sand, and had no foundation? No. Such a house would not be fit to live in. But trust in God is as important to us as the foundation is to the building.

Now I wish to speak to you of *four* things for which we should trust in God.

The first thing for which we should learn to trust God is OUR DAILY BREAD.

Jesus taught us to pray for this in the Lord's prayer, when we are directed to say —"Our Father....give us this day our daily bread." And whatever God teaches us to pray for, He intends that we should trust Him to give us. What a beautiful lesson Jesus taught His disciples on this subject, one day when He was on earth! Most of them had been fishermen. They had been accustomed to earn their food and clothing by hard work. And when they had caught a good lot of fish, they knew very well how to sell them, and get money to buy bread, and clothes for their families. But now they had given up their fishing business to follow Jesus,—to preach the gospel, and as He said, become "fishers of men." And I suppose they began to be afraid they never would get money enough to buy themselves bread to eat, or clothes to put on. And so in the very first sermon that Jesus preached—the sermon on the mount, He gave them a most beautiful lesson on this subject; a lesson which I suppose they never forgot. He said to them—"Take no thought for your life, what ye shall eat, or what ye shall drink; nor yet for your bodies what ye shall put on. Behold the fowls of the air; for they sow not, neither do they reap, nor gather into barns; yet your heavenly Father feedeth them. Are ye not much better than they ?" What a sweet lesson this is to trust in God for our daily bread! Every time we see a little bird, hopping about, picking up the food which God has provided for it, chirping cheerfully, and singing merrily, we should be reminded of the lesson Jesus gave His disciples. That little bird becomes a sort of preacher,—a minister of Christ to us. He seems to say—"Don't be afraid. Trust God for your daily bread. I have no money. I can't work for my food, yet, somehow or other God always sees that I get enough to eat. The God who takes care of a tiny little thing like me, won't forget you. If he feeds His birds, surely He won't starve his children."

This is the lesson Jesus gives us about our daily food. And then see what He says about trusting God for clothing. "Consider the lilies of the field, how they grow: they toil not, neither do they spin: and yet I say unto you that even Solomon, in all his glory, was not arrayed like one of these. Wherefore, if God so clothe the grass of the field, which to day is, and to-morrow is cast into the oven, shall He not much more clothe you, O, ye of little faith?" Here Jesus does, as it were, ordain every spear of grass, and every beautiful flower that springs out of the earth, and make them preachers. When we see them covering the ground, and adorning it with beauty, they seem to say to us—"O trust in God for clothing. For surely He who can afford to clothe His field in such a way, will never forget to clothe his people."

Let us think of these precious lessons of Jesus whenever we look upon the little birds, the grass, or the flowers, and they will help us to trust in God for our daily bread.

You remember the prophet Elijah. He had to go out, and live all by himself in the wilderness, because Ahab, the wicked king of Israel, was trying to kill him. There was nothing there for him to eat. It was impossible for him to get any food for himself. But he trusted in God, and He sent him ravens to bring him bread and flesh morning by morning, and evening by evening, just as long as he stayed there. We are not told exactly how long this was, but it must have been a good many months. How very wonderful this was! You must recollect that it was during a time of famine. Food was very scarce. The ravens must have found it hard to get food for themselves. And then they are very greedy birds, as their name indicates. They are called *ravens* because of their *ravenous* disposition. They are eager to devour all they can get. No doubt these ravens were very hungry, and yet they brought this food, and laid it down at the feet of the prophet, without attempting to eat a bite of it. O, it is worth while to trust for our daily bread in that God who could feed one of His people in such a way!

Perhaps you have heard the story about "The Man-Raven," but it suits so nicely this part of our subject, that I must bring it in here.

Mrs. Rogers was a poor woman, living in a small town in England. She had four little children, of whom Richard, the eldest, was about eight years old. One evening, in the midst of winter, her children were hungry. She had no food to give them. But she loved and served God, and trusting in Him to provide for them daily bread, she kneeled down with her hungry little ones, to tell Him of their wants, and ask Him to supply them.

At the close of the prayer, Richard said to her, "Mother, doesn't the Bible say that God once sent some ravens with bread to a man who was hungry?"

"Yes, my child; but that was a long time ago. And that was a miracle, and we've no right to expect that God will work miracles now."

"Well, but," said Richard, "don't you think God can send us some ravens with bread now, just as well as He did then? I'm going to open the door, or they can't get in;" and jumping up, he ran to the door, and threw it open wide, so that the candle shone out into the street.

A few minutes after, the village magistrate was passing by, and glancing through the open door, he was so pleased by the sight of the mother surrounded by her little ones, and all looking so neat and clean, that he stepped in and said to Mrs. Rogers—"My good friend, how does it happen that your door is standing open this cold winter's night?"

Mrs. Rogers was a little confused at seeing such a gentleman come into her poor room; but she rose up, and spoke respectfully to him, and taking off Richard's cap, and laying her hand on his head, she said, smiling—

"It was my little boy that opened the door, a moment ago, in order, as he said, 'that the ravens might come in, and bring us some bread.'"

Now the ravens, you know, are always black birds, and it so happened that this gentleman was actually dressed in black, from head to foot.

"Ah, indeed," said he, laughing, "Richard is right. The raven has come, and he is a pretty big one, too. Come with me, my little man, and I will show you where the bread is."

Then he took the little boy with him to the grocer's, filled a basket with provisions, and sent him home with it. Richard, you may be sure, hurried back as fast as he could. The poor children were soon clapping their hands with joy at the sight of the food.

When they had finished their meal, Richard again went to the door, took off his cap, and looking up to the sky, said, "Thank you, dear Father in heaven, for sending this nice food." Then he came in, and shut the door. "Whoso trusteth in the Lord, happy is he." The first thing for which we ought to trust God is, *for daily bread.*

The second thing for which we should trust God is, PROTECTION IN DANGER.

We read in the Bible about the great danger that Daniel was in. If he didn't stop praying, he would be thrown into the den of hungry lions. But Daniel resolved to go on praying, and trust to God to protect him from the lions. He continued to pray three times a day, and when he was thrown into the lions' den, God shut the mouths of the lions so that they didn't hurt him the least.

Then there were those three good men, Shadrack, Mesheck, and Abednego, who were in danger of being thrown into the burning fiery furnace, unless they would kneel down and worship the golden image which Nebuchadnezzar the king had set up. But they knew it was a great sin to bow down before that stupid image. They resolved not to commit this sin. They made up their minds to do what was right, and then trust to God to take care of them, and protect them from danger. They did so: and when they were thrown into the blazing furnace, God kept the flames from hurting them; and they walked up and down in the midst of the roaring fire as safely and pleasantly as if they had been walking in their own garden. How wonderful this was! What an illustration of the truth of Solomon's words when he said, "Whoso trusteth the Lord, happy is he."

In the year 1665, nearly two hundred years ago, the great city of London was visited by the plague. This was a dreadful disease, like the cholera, or the yellow fever, only worse than either of them. None of the physicians could cure it, or do anything for the relief of those who had it. The people were cut down before it, just as the grass is mowed down by the scythe. There was a good minister living in London when this plague broke out, whose name was the Rev. Thomas Vincent. He had no Church of his own, but had been occupied as a teacher. When this dreadful disease began he shut np his school, and resolved to spend his time in preaching to the people, in visiting the sick, and dying, and telling them about Jesus. Most of the clergy had left, and his friends tried to persuade him to go away too, and not to expose himself to so much danger. But he refused to go. He said he trusted in God: He was able to protect him from the danger if He saw fit, and if not he was willing to die in the work that was before him. And so he stayed there all the time of the plague. He preached in some of the Churches every Sunday. Great crowds flocked to hear him, for all business was stopped. During the week he went everywhere among the sick, reading and talking to them, and telling them about Jesus, and the way to heaven. During that terrible season nearly 70,000 people died of the plague in London. Seven persons died in the family in which this good minister lived. Yet he did not die. He never was sick an hour the whole time. He trusted in God, and happy was he. God protected him in danger.

I wish to give you one other illustration of this part of the subject. This is connected with the late war. It took place at the battle of Gettysburgh, in our own State, in the summer of 1863.

In one of the regiments of the rebel army was a company of soldiers from North Carolina. In this company was a person who belonged to the religious Society of Friends, sometimes called Quakers. He had been forced to join the army against his own will. He protested against it, and said he was opposed, on conscientious principles, to fighting, under any circumstances; that he could not and would not fight. But nobody would mind him. He was forced to shoulder his musket, and march. He did so, but always saying that he would not fight.

The regiment to which he belonged joined General Lee's army in the invasion of Pennsylvania. But it never was called into action till they came to Gettysburgh. There it was soon known that a great battle was to be fought. Just before the battle began this Friend went to the Colonel of his regiment and said he could not go into the fight. The Colonel said he must. He said he could not, and would not. "Then," said the Colonel, "I'll have you shot."

"Thee can do as thee pleases about that. I trust in God—but I cannot fight."

The Colonel had him led out into an open space, and ordered out a squad of soldiers to shoot him. While the soldiers were making ready, taking aim, and waiting the com mand to fire—the man stood calmly there, and lifting up his face to heaven, said in a loud, clear voice—"Father forgive them, for they know not what they do!" The men threw down their arms, and said "they wouldn't shoot such a man."

Another squad was called out, and the same thing occured with them. The Colonel was very angry. He swore a dreadful oath declaring he would trample the man to death. He put his spurs to his horse, and galloped up to him to ride him down. But when the horse came up to the man, he reared up on his hind legs and turned away from him. This was repeated two or three times with the same result. Then the trumpet sounded to battle.

The Colonel had to hasten away and lead his men into the fight, and in one of the first valleys fired by our army he fell mortally wounded. The Quaker soldier was taken prisoner by our men. He was brought to Philadelphia and afterwards discharged by President Lincoln, and released from doing military duty. This man "trusted in the Lord, and happy was he." The second thing for which we should trust God is—*protection in danger.**

The third thing for which we should trust God is COMFORT IN SORROW.

God has two ways of comforting His people when they are in sorrow. One of these ways is by *taking away the cause of their sorrow.* One day God sent the prophet Isaiah to Hezekiah, the king of Judah, to tell him that he was was soon to die, and

---

* NOTE. The facts of this incident are perfectly authentic. Several of my intimate friends, intelligent, and reliable Christian men, who are personally acquainted with the friends of the individual referred to, have furnished me with the above account, and have repeatedly certified me of its correctness. R. N.

that he must get ready at once for death. This threw him into great trouble. He didn't want to leave his kingdom just then, and he felt a very great desire to live a few years longer. He wept, and prayed, and was in great sorrow. God heard his prayers, and sent the prophet to him again to tell him that he might live fifteen years longer. Then the king was very glad, and went up into the temple to thank God for His great goodness. Thus you see how God comforted Isaiah by taking away the cause of his sorrow.

Some years ago, during the wars between England and France, an English ship was captured by the French, and the officers and crew were taken prisoners. The captain of the English ship was named Harris. He was a Christian man, and knew how to trust in God. But when he found himself a prisoner in a strange land, his vessel lost, and all his property taken from him, he was greatly distressed. He couldn't eat the prison fare, and yet he had no money to buy any other. He feared he should get sick and die, and thus his heart was full of sorrow. But though he felt so badly, he never said a word about it to his fellow prisoners. He only lifted up his heart in prayer to God, and tried to trust in Him.

One day a French gentleman came into the prison, and made this singular statement. Said he:—"There is some person in this prison in great distress of mind for want of money. I don't know who it is, or what his name is; but the moment I see him I shall know him, for I dreamed about him last night, and saw him so distinctly in my dream that I shall recognize him at once."

He then began to look round among the prisoners, and the very moment he saw Captain Harris, he exclaimed, "That's the man." He then inquired if he was not in want of money, and lent him as much as he needed. Captain Harris "trusted in the Lord, and happy was he." God comforted him by removing the cause of his sorrow.

But God doesn't always see it best to take

away from His people the thing that troubles them. Then he has another way of comforting them. He does this *by helping them to bear their troubles comfortably.* Suppose you are carrying a heavy load on your shoulder. You want to get rest. Well, now, if a strong man should come along, and take hold of the other end of the load so that you could hardly feel it, that would be about the same as though it were lifted entirely off your shoulder.

St. Paul had a trouble of some kind when he was on earth. He called it "a thorn in the flesh." We don't know what it was. But it worried him a great deal, and he prayed to God three times to take it away. God did not do this; but He told him He would give him grace to help him bear it. This comforted Paul in his sorrow, as much as if the cause of it had been taken away.

There was a good minister in London once, who did not fully understand what he was preaching about. He felt that a true Christian ought to be happy at all times, but still he didn't exactly see how that could be in a world where there is so much trouble. He prayed very earnestly that God would help him to understand it. One day, after he had done praying, he felt that it pressed upon his mind very strongly, that if he would take a walk over the Waterloo bridge he would get some information on the subject. He went to the bridge. When he was about half way across, he overtook a plain-looking man, dressed in very poor clothes.

"I wish you a good morning, my friend," said the minister.

"I never had a bad morning, sir," replied the man.

"That is very singular. I wish you may always be so fortunate."

"I never was unfortunate," said he.

"I hope you will always be as happy," said the minister.

"I never was unhappy," said the other.

"I wish," said the minister, "that you would explain yourself a little."

"That I will do cheerfully," said he. "I

said that I never had a bad morning, for every morning, even if I am pinched with hunger, brings me something for which to thank God. And while I have cause for praise, whether it rains, or hails, or snows, no morning comes to me without joy. If I am poor and miserable in this world's concerns, I can yet thank God for loving me, and giving me His grace. You wished that I might always be fortunate; but I cannot be unfortunate, because nothing befalls me but according to the will of God, and I believe that His will is always good in whatever He does, or permits to be done. You wished me always happy; but I cannot be unhappy, because my will is always resigned to the will of God." This man "trusted in God, and happy was he." *The third thing for which we trust God is, comfort in sorrow.*

There is one more thing for which we should trust God, but this is the most important of all, viz:—TO SAVE OUR SOULS.

The Bible tells us that the way to be saved

is "to believe on the Lord Jesus Christ." To believe in Jesus, or to have faith in Jesus, means the same thing as to have trust in Him. When Jesus hung bleeding and dying on the cross, He was suffering the punishment of our sins. And because he has suffered for us, we have nothing to suffer. We are pardoned and saved when we believe in Jesus, or when we trust in Him to save us.

I was reading the other day, about two little children. They were brother and sister. Their names were Charles and Jane. They loved each other very much, and were generally good children. But sometimes they gave way to bad tempers, and then they had to be punished.

One day little Jane, who was only about four years old, had been doing something wrong. To punish her for this, her mother told her she couldn't go out to play, but must sit still in the corner of the nursery for half an hour. Presently Charles came in. He was a year older than Jane. Finding that his sister had to be punished for doing wrong, he said—"Mother, please let me sit in Janie's place, and take her punishment for her." His mother was pleased at his kindness, and said he might. Then he ran up to his sister and kissed her, and said, "Now, Janie, *you* may go and play, and I will stay here in your place." When Janie was gone, he settled himself quietly down in a corner of the room, and seemed to be engaged in thinking earnestly about something. After a while he said, "Mother, isn't this like Jesus?" "What do you mean, my child?" asked his mother. "Why, didn't Jesus take our punishment when he hung upon the cross, that we might not be punished forever, just as I have taken Janie's punishment?"

That little fellow was right. He understood the Bible way of salvation. His sister was out playing because he was bearing her punishment. And just so we are saved because Jesus has borne our punishment. The Bible tells us "He was wounded for our transgressions, and bruised for our iniquities: and by His stripes we are healed." All that is necessary for us in order to be saved, is to *trust in Jesus.* This is what Jesus meant when He said, "God so loved the world that He gave His only begotten Son that *whosoever believeth in Him* should not perish, but have everlasting life." "Whosoever believeth"—or trusteth—in Jesus, "shall have everlasting life." Jesus has done everything for us. There is nothing left for us to do but to trust. It is not our tears or prayers that save us. It is not being baptised or receiving the Lord's Supper that saves us. It is Jesus who saves us. He saves all who trust in Him. Many people won't believe this. They think they must do something themselves before Jesus will save them. But this is a mistake. And we never can be happy till we give up trying to do anything, and just trust to Jesus.

I was reading lately of a lady who felt that she was a sinner. She was in great distress on account of her sins. She went to her minister, and asked, "What must I *do* to be saved?" He said, "There is nothing for you to do. Only trust in Jesus, and He will save you."

But she thought there must be something for her to do. She went home. She shut herself up in her room, and resolved to keep on reading her Bible and praying, till she could feel that her sins were pardoned, and she was saved.

After awhile she felt very tired, and fell asleep. Then she dreamed that she was falling over a frightful precipice. But just as she was going over she caught hold of a twig, by which she hung over the yawning gulf. In her fright she cried out, "O save me! save me!"

She heard a voice below, which, in her dream, she knew to be the voice of Jesus. He said, "Let go the twig, and I will save you." "Lord, save me!" she cried again and again. Still the same answer was returned—"Let go the twig, and I will save you." She thought she would fall and perish if she loosed her hold on the twig. But the same earnest, solemn voice, was heard saying, "I cannot save you till you let go that twig." At last she let it go. Then she fell into the arms of Jesus, and was safe. The joy which this occasioned, woke her. In her sleep she had learned the way of salvation. She found that the things she was trying to do, in order to be saved, were like the twig to which she clung, and which kept her from being saved. And when she gave up trying to do anything, and just trusted in Jesus, this was like letting go the twig, and falling into His arms. Then she was saved. This is the meaning of that beautiful hymn we often sing:—

"Rock of Ages, cleft for me,
Let me hide myself in Thee:
In my hand no price I bring,
Simply to Thy cross I cling."

Now I have spoken of four things for which we should trust in God. We should trust Him *for our daily bread*:—for *protection in danger*:—*for comfort in sorrow*:—and *to save our souls.*

But we never can trust God aright, unless He shall help us. Then let us ask God in prayer to give us His grace and Holy Spirit that we may know how to trust Him. Then we shall understand the meaning of the text when it says—"Whoso trusteth in the Lord, happy is he."

IX.

The Blessing of Meekness.

"Blessed are the meek."

MATTHEW v. 5.

IX.

"Blessed are the meek."
MATTHEW v. 5.

THESE words are found in the Sermon on the Mount. That was our Saviour's first sermon. It was the greatest sermon ever preached. What a wonderful preacher Jesus was! For four thousand years before He came His coming had been foretold. That was a long time to wait for His coming. It was so long that some people began to think He never would come at all. But, at last He came. And then His friends felt a very great desire to know what He would say when He began to preach. When the time arrived for Him to preach His first sermon, He didn't enter a church and stand up in a pulpit: but He went up to the top a mountain. The people followed Him there, and gathered round Him, very anxious to hear His sermon. Then He sat down, with the people all about Him, in the open air, on the mountain top, and preached this wonderful sermon. You would think it very strange, if I should have a chair here, and sit down to preach. And it would be strange because the custom with us is for ministers to stand up, when they preach. But then, it was different. The custom then was for ministers, or public teachers to sit down, when they were preaching, or teaching. And so we read that Jesus "sat down" to preach. And when He began His sermon the first thing He had to speak about was blessings. The very first word that came out of His mouth when He began to preach was the word—"*Blessed.*" And He went on to repeat that sweet word—blessed—blessed—blessed—till He had used it nine, or ten times before He had anything else to say. It seemed as if His great loving heart was so full of blessings that there was nothing else for Him to speak of. The

Bible tells us that God sent Him into our world to bless men, and here we see what a good beginning He made in this blessed work. But the things that Jesus spoke of as blessings, are very different from those that people generally regard as blessings. Most people say—" blessed are they that are rich" : but Jesus says " blessed are the poor in spirit." Most people say,—" blessed are they that are always glad," but Jesus says, " blessed are they that mourn, for they shall be comforted." Most people say,—" blessed are they that always have plenty to eat, and drink, and never feel the want of anything," but Jesus says,—" blessed are they that *hunger* and *thirst* after righteousness." Most people say,—" blessed are those who stand up for their own rights, and are always ready to give sharp answers to any who speak sharply to them" : but Jesus says, " blessed are the meek."

Some ministers don't try to practice what they preach. You have often seen sign-posts by the side of the road. They are planted there, and point to people with the finger, the way to walk in, but they never move in it themselves. And ministers who preach what they don't practice are sign-post ministers. They point out a way which *they* don't travel. But it was not so with Jesus. *He preached* meekness, and He *practised* meekness. Here, He says "blessed are the meek." And in another place He says—"Learn of me, for *I am* meek." And, O, Jesus was wonderfully meek. He never spoke a cross, or unkind word to any body. And yet how many things were said to Him that were calculated to hurt His feelings, and make Him angry! They called Him a glutton, and a drunkard. And when He performed wonderous miracles by His own power, they said He did them by the help of Satan. Yet we read that "when He was reviled He reviled not again." When they said all manner of evil things about Him, "like a sheep before the shearers He opened not His mouth." Jesus might well say, "Learn of me, for I am meek." To be meek is to be like Jesus. Meek persons are always gentle, and kind, and polite in the way in which they speak and act to others. And in His great sermon on the Mount Jesus said "*Blessed* are the meek." I wish to speak of *three* ways in which meekness brings a blessing even in this present life.

The first way is BY SAVING US FROM TROUBLE.

Sometimes we hear persons complaining that the people around them are cross, or disagreeable, when the real trouble lies in themselves.

One day a little boy, whose name was Johnny Wilson, came running into the house when his sister Mary was sewing. He held something in his hand which he had found in the yard. "Oh, sister Mary," said he, "I've found a pretty thing. It is a piece of red glass, and when I look through it every thing is red too. The trees, the houses, the green grass, your face, and everything is red."

Mary said, "Yes, it's very beautiful: and let me show you how to learn a useful lesson from it. You remember the other day, you thought everybody was cross to you. Then you were like this piece of glass, which makes everything look red, because *it* is red. When you feel cross and disagreeable you think everybody around you is cross and disagreeable too. But when you are in good humor, and feel kind, and pleasant yourself, other people will seem just the same towards you.

I remember hearing of a little boy who was taught this same lesson by his mother in a different way. They were on a visit in the country. At the edge of the woods, near the house when they were staying, was a very fine echo. Little George didn't understand about echoes. One day his mother was sitting on the porch, and he was playing near by. Something led him to call aloud. Presently the echo of his voice came back. He didn't know what it was, but supposed that some boy in the woods was calling to him. He stood still awhile.

Then he cried "Halloo!" "Halloo," was the reply. "Who are you?"—"Who are you?" asked the echo. "Clear out!" —"Clear out." "You're a mean chap!"— "Mean chap."

"I'll lick you!"—"Lick you," said the echo. He couldn't stand this. So he ran to the house. "Mother, I don't want to stay here," said he, "there's som bad boy down in the woods who keeps calling me names, and threatening to whip me."

"O, I guess not," said his mother, who had heard it all, and knew what it was.

"Yes, indeed there is then, for he has been calling me names, and saying saucy things to me."

"Well, go out again," said his mother, "and tell him he's a good fellow, and ask him to have an apple."

So the little boy ran out towards the woods, and cried "Halloo!"—"Halloo" was echoed back. "You're a good fellow." "Good fellow," was the answer. "I'll give you an apple."—"Give an apple"—was heard from the woods. Then he ran back to his mother, and said, "Why, mother, there must be two boys in the woods, a good boy, and a bad boy."

"No, my child," said his mother, "there is no boy there at all. It's only the echo of your own voice that you have heard. When you speak kind and pleasant words, the echoes are kind and pleasant. And when you speak cross, and ugly words the echoes you hear are just the same. Kindness is like a soft, gentle echo. If we speak loving words to others, loving words will come back to us, and if we do kind actions to others kind actions will come back to us."

A great while ago there was a little girl at school in France. One day she was walking with her companions in one of the public gardens in Paris. It happened that there was a poor soldier then on duty. He was suffering very much from thirst, but was not able to leave his post to go and get a drink. So he begged these young ladies to bring him a drink of water from a fountain not far off. The little girl's companions passed proudly on, and said it was very rude and impertinent in a common soldier to speak to them. But little Lucy had a kind and tender heart, full of meekness and gentleness, and she couldn't think of leaving a fellow-creature to want, when it was in her power to help him. So, she ran, and got some water, though her companions were scolding her for doing it. When she brought the water to the poor soldier, he drank it eagerly, and then thanked her heartily for it, and asked her to give him her name, and the name of the street and the number of the house in which she lived. She did this, and then went away.

Not long after this a dreadful massacre took place in that city, of all the Protestants. Hundreds and thousands of them were cruelly murdered! But that little girl was saved. The poor soldier had not forgotten her. He had been accustomed to scenes of cruelty and bloodshed, but that one kind action had made a deep impression on him. He sought out the little girl while the massacre was going on, and took her to a place of safety. And so she found that the echo of her kindness and gentleness came back to her amidst those fearful scenes of slaughter. Here you see how her meekness was a blessing to her in saving her from trouble.

Now let me tell you about the conductor of a railway train, and the trouble he got into by not having a meek, or gentle, pleasant way of speaking. The cars were waiting at a station on one of our western railways. The baggage master was busy with baggage and checks. The men were hurrying to and fro with chests and trunks. Men, women and children were rushing for the cars, and securing their seats, while the engine was snorting, and puffing and blowing.

A man very poorly dressed was standing on the platform. He was looking carelessly about. He was lame, and, judging from his personal appearance, one would have supposed he was a person of no wealth or influence. The conductor slapped him roughly on the shoulder, and said, "Halloo, old Limpy; get on board, or you'll be left."

"Time enough, I reckon," said he, and continued quietly looking about him.

Presently the last trunk was tumbled into the baggage car. "All aboard," cried the conductor. "Get on, Limpy," said he to the carelessly dressed lame man, as he passed by.

He said nothing, but quietly stepped on to the platform of the last car, as the train was slowly moving off. He took a seat, and put his valise in the rack overhead.

After the train had moved on a few miles, the conductor came in. Passing along, he recognized the lame man, and said in a very rough way—

"Hand out your money here."

"I don't pay," said the man, very quietly.

"Don't pay?"

"No, sir."

"Well, sir, then I shall put you out at the next station," and he seized the valise in the rack over his head.

"Better not be so rough, young man," replied the stranger.

The conductor left the valise there while he went on collecting the fare or tickets from the other passengers. As he stopped at a seat a little way off, a gentleman, who had heard what had just been said, looked up at him, and asked, "Do you know who that person is to whom you have been speaking?"

"No, sir."

"Well, that's Mr. Warburton, the president of this road."

"Are you sure of that, sir?" said the conductor, trying to conceal his agitation.

"Oh, yes. I know know him very well."

If a thunder-bolt had struck him he could hardly have been more confounded. He was ashamed and mortified at himself, as well as grieved to think of being turned out of his place. For of course he had nothing better to expect after insulting the president of the Company in such a manner. But he went through the cars, and finished the business of collecting the fares or tickets. Then he came back to Mr. Warburton. He took his books from his pocket, the bank bills and the tickets he had collected, and laid them in Mr. Warburton's hands, saying, at the same time,

"I resign my place, sir."

The President looked over the accounts a few moments, and then, motioning to a vacant seat at his side, said;—

"Sit down, sir, I would like to talk with you."

As the young man sat down, the President turned to him a face on which there was no trace of anger, and said, in an undertone;—

"My young friend, I'm so sorry to see you act in such a way. I have no revenge to gratify in this matter, but you have been very imprudent. If you should act in this way to strangers, it would do a great injury to the company. I might tell the Board of Managers of what has taken place, but I won't. By doing this, I should throw you out of a situation and you might find hard to get another. But in future remember to be gentle and polite to all you meet. You cannot judge a man by the coat he wears, and even the poorest ought to be treated with kindness. Take back your books, sir. I shan't tell any one of what has passed. If you change your course, nothing that has happened shall injure you. Your situation is still continued. Good morning, sir."

The train of cars went thundering on its way, but that rough young conductor had been taught a lesson that he would not be likely soon to forget. If we could have gone to him at the close of that day, and have asked him what Jesus meant when He said, "Blessed are the meek"? he would have given us a good illustration of His meaning. He would have told us of the trouble that he brought upon himself by the want of meekness, and in what a blessed way the meekness of the President of that railway had saved him from that trouble.

The first way in which meekness is a blessing is, *by saving us from trouble.*

The second way in which it is a blessing is, by DOING GOOD TO OURSELVES.

Meekness, or gentleness, is very much despised by some people, yet it is one of the mightiest things in the world. God is conquering the world to Himself by love, the love of Jesus in dying for us. And gentleness or meekness is the only way in which love shows itself in acting or speaking. A kind word, a loving, gentle voice or manner, has more power in it than all the harsh words that ever were spoken, or all the hard blows that can be given. It will subdue the stubborn will, smooth down the rugged, frowning brow, and work wonders. Why, even the dumb animals, though they don't understand what you say, yet know when you speak kindly to them.

A man was driving a loaded cart along the street one day. It was a heavy load the horse was drawing. At one place he didn't turn in the way the carter wanted him to go. He was a cross, ill-tempered man, and he began to swear at the horse, and lash him with his whip. Still he wouldn't go right. The more the man beat him, the more he persisted in rearing and plunging, and holding back. There was another man along with the cart of a different temper. He went up to the horse, and patted him on the neck. He stroked his mane softly, and spoke gently to him. The horse turned his head, and fixed his big eyes on the man, just as if he was trying to say, "Why, my good fellow, I'll do anything in the world for *you*, because you speak kindly to me." And then, bending his broad chest against the load, he turned the cart down the lane, and trotted along as briskly as though the load was only a plaything.

I said that politeness is one of the forms in which true meekness, or gentleness, shows itself. Now it costs very little to be polite, and it often pays very well. Some years ago, there was a poor widow in one of our

Southern States. She had an only son whose name was George. She was a Christian mother, and had taught her son the blessedness of meekness. He was a very gentle, polite little fellow, and pretty smart, too. One evening George's mother wanted to milk their cow. But the cow had a calf, who didn't like to see anybody getting the milk but herself, and would therefore make all the trouble she could while this operation was going on. So George's mother told him to him to catch the calf, and hold it by the ears till she had done milking. He did so. And while he was thus engaged, a very wealthy gentleman in the neighborhood was passing by. As he rode along, he said—

"Good evening, my little man."

"Good evening, sir," said George, at the same time making a polite bow.

"But why didn't you pull off your hat, my son," asked the gentleman, "with such a polite bow?"

"Why, sir, you see I am holding the calf by the ears, while mother milks the cow;

but if you will only have the kindness to come and hold her for me, I will take my hat off in a minute."

The gentleman was so pleased with George's politeness, and the shrewdness of his reply, that not long after he came to see his mother. He said to her—" My friend, your little George is a smart boy, and if he is properly trained he'll make a great man some day. If you will allow me, I shall be glad to educate him, and give him a good start in the world."

The mother thanked the gentleman for his kindness, and let him take charge of her son. And George rose from the ears of that calf to the highest rank as a lawyer; he was sent to the Legislature; then to Congress; and finally he became the Governor of the State. This was George McDuffie, the Governor of South Carolina. *George's polite bow made his fortune.*

Let me tell you another story that relates to a gentleman in this city. It shows how much good we may do to ourselves, by be ing gentle, and pleasant in our manners. And if we learn of Jesus to be meek we shall always be gentle and pleasant.

Some years ago two gentlemen,—one of whom was a foreigner,—visited the different locomotive workshops in this city. They first went to that large one out Broad Street. They asked permission to go through the establishment, and see all the different parts of it. But they were not kindly received: no pains were taken to give them the information which they wanted, and they left the place disappointed. They went to several other large establishments, and were treated in the same way. At last they were led to a machine shop, on a much smaller scale. The owner of this factory superintended it himself. He was a very skilful mechanic. He was a man of very kind, gentle manners. He received the gentlemen very pleasantly. He took the greatest pains to show them all about his workshops, and explained everything to them that they wanted to know. And when they went away they were fully satisfied not only that he was a very obliging, gentlemanly man, but also that he was a most excellent workman, and understood his business thoroughly.

Well, not very long after this, that man was surprised to receive an invitation from Nicholas, the Emperor of Russia, to go to St. Petersburgh, the capital of his empire. It seemed that the emperor was anxious to introduce railways and locomotives into Russia. He wished to get a first-rate machinist to make locomotives for him. So he sent an agent to this country to find out one of the best makers of locomotives. One of those two gentlemen was the emperor's agent. He came to this city to examine our workshops. He made choice of a Philadelphia mechanic to recommend to the emperor. He invited him to move his factory to St. Petersburgh. He did so. He remained there a number of years, building locomotives for the emperor. Then he returned home. He is living in this city now, one of our richest men. But he owes it all to the kindness and gentleness with which he received those two strangers.

"Aunty," said a little girl, "I believe I have found a new key to unlock people's hearts, and make them willing to do what I ask; for you know, Aunty, God took away my father and mother, and they want people to be kind to their poor little daughter."

"What is the key," asked her Aunty.

"It's only one little word—guess what?" But Aunty was no guesser.

"It is *please*," said the child; "Aunty, it is please. If I ask one of the big girls at school, 'Please show me my parsing lesson?' she says, 'O, yes,' and helps me. If I ask, 'Sarah, please do this for me?' no matter what it is, she takes her hands out of the suds, and does it. If I say, 'Please, Uncle, do this for me,' he says, 'Yes, Pussy, if I can.' And if I say, 'Please, Aunty—'

"Well, what does Aunty do?" asked Aunty herself. "Oh, you look and *smile just like Mother*, and that is the best of all," said the little girl, throwing her arms round her Aunty's neck, while a tear filled her eye.

Now that gentle hearted little girl was finding, in her every-day life, the meaning of our Saviour's words when he said, "Blessed are the meek." She found that blessing in the good that her meekness did to herself.

And that new key which she used, is one which grown people may use as well as children. Everybody has heard of the Duke of Wellington. He was the greatest soldier England has had in this century. He whipped the great Napoleon Bonaparte at the battle of Waterloo. When this great warrior had done fighting, and had retired to private life, he was as meek and gentle as a little child. He was very fond of using this little girl's new key. He always said, "If you please," when he asked for anything. He had been accustomed to command large armies, and to give orders that no one dared to disobey, and yet "If you please," was constantly on his lips. It is said they were the last words he ever spoke. There the great warrior, the "iron duke," as he was called, is on his death bed. A faithful servant is attending him. He thinks the Duke is thirsty. He pours out a little tea in a saucer and asks him if he will have a drink. "Yes, if you please." He never spoke again. All about him loved him because he was so meek and gentle. "Blessed are the meek." The second way in which meekness is a blessing is, *by doing good to ourselves.*

The third way in which it is a blessing is, BY DOING GOOD TO OTHERS.

This is one of the ways of doing good which we can all practice. There are some ways of doing good that only rich people can practice. But we can't all be rich, and so we can't all do good in those ways. There are other ways of doing good that only great people can practice. But we can't all be great, and therefore we can't all do good in those ways. But we can all try to be meek and gentle, kind and loving in what we say and d ; and so this is a way in which we can all be engaged in doing good. And it is one of the best ways of doing good.

See, there is a poor sick and wounded soldier. He has been taken from the battle-field, and put into an ambulance to be carried to the hospital. But that hospital is a good way off, and it will take him a good while to reach it. As soon as the ambulance begins to move, it is found that the wheels are dry, and every time they move round they make a terrible creaking, grinding noise. The springs are broken under it, too, and it goes jolting and jarring over the rough roads. Ah! how the harsh noise of the creaking wheels distresses the aching head of that poor soldier! And what terrible pain the jolting causes to his wounded limb! But presently some kind agent of the Christian or Sanitary Commission comes along. He puts some grease on the wheels of the ambulance, and that stops their creaking. He has the broken springs taken off, and new ones put in their place, and now the poor soldier goes softly along, with no noise, and no jolting to trouble him.

And this is just the way in which a meek or gentle spirit is trying to do good to others all the time. It is always trying to stop the creaking and jolting that worry people as they are journeying on through this world.

Let me show you how much good was once done by a meek man to a person who was very angry with him.

This person had a very violent temper. He had a dispute with an acquaintance of his who was a profe sor of religion, and who had done him an injury. He was very angry with this Christian man, and went to see him for the purpose of having a quarrel with him. When he got to his house, he said, in a very angry way, "Sir, I've come to tell you that you have injured me very much by what you did the other day."

He was just going to begin to scold and abuse him; but the Christian man headed him off by saying, "My friend, it was very wrong in me to do so. I am truly sorry for it. I ask your forgiveness, and I will gladly do anything in my power to make amends for the injury I have done."

But this was what the angry man did not expect. He was not prepared for it. It took him, as the sailors say, "all aback." He was obliged to say that he was satisfied, and go away feeling vexed and mortified that he had not had an opportunity to say all the angry and bitter things that he had gone there to say.

On his way home, however, he began to talk to himself in this way: "What a strange man this is! I didn't expect he would act so. I thought he'd say something sharp to me, and then I'd have a chance to give him a regular blowing up. If any body had spoken to me as I spoke to him, I should have been dreadful angry. If it's his religion that does this for him, it certainly makes him a much better man than I am. There must be something in religion. I'd better look into it."

He *did* look into it. The result was that

he soon became a Christian himself. And it was the meekness and gentleness of that Christian friend that led to this happy change. Jesus said—"Blessed are the meek!" And here, in the good they do to others, we see how it is that the meek are blessed.

Now let me tell you how kindness changed the whole character of a bad boy. Miss Mason was a young lady who lived in Connecticut. Her father died, and she was obliged to do something for her own living. She had been educated for a teacher. There was a school at Westbrook, not far from where she lived, without a teacher. She applied for the situation and got it. But she had never taught before, and she felt very awkward and timid in taking charge of a large school. There were a number of big boys in the school. One of them, Joe Stanton, was the worst boy in the neighborhood. He was a poor orphan boy, rude and neglected, and the ringleader of the other boys in all mischief. The first day that Miss Mason took charge of the school, he gave her more trouble than all the other boys put together. He didn't mind what she said. He was setting an example of disobedience to the whole school, and playing all sorts of tricks. Poor Miss Mason! she was very much discouraged, and didn't know what to do. Joe Stanton was too big a boy for her to undertake to punish, and yet she felt she never could get on unless something was done to make him behave better. She resolved to try the effect of kindness on him. So, at the close of the afternoon, she asked him, very pleasantly, to stay after the school was dismissed, and help her shut up the school. He said he would. The shutters were closed, and the door locked, and as she turned to go home, Joe walked along with her. As they went on, Miss Mason said ;—

"Have you any sister, Joseph?" This touched the only tender spot in his rough heart.

"I had one once," he said; "little Mary; she was my only sister. I used to take care of her, and play with her, and carry her out of doors, and draw her in the wagon I made for her; and she loved me more than any one else did, and always used to run to the door and meet me when I came home. But she's dead, and nobody cares for me now. She had a fever, and didn't know me when I spoke to her, and in just a week she died. Her grave is right over there, and perhaps you'd like to see it some time?"

"Yes, Joseph, let's walk over there now," said the teacher. They went slowly along, still talking about little Mary. They reached the grave, and sat down on a stone near it. Joe had been wiping away the tears as they trickled down his cheeks, one by one. But now the fountain of his grief was broken up, and he could control himself no longer. He covered his face with his hands, as he sobbed and wept aloud.

"Oh! she's dead! she's dead!" he cried; and nobody cares for me now."

"Yes, Joseph, I'll care care for you," said the teacher, as she laid her hand gently on his uncovered head. Then she spoke to him of Jesus, who is the friend of the fatherless, and of that blessed heaven, to which He will take those who love Him, and where they will meet their friends again. And then she told him of her own sorrow,—of the loss of her father,—how lonely she felt in the world, —how she had to work for her living now,— and how hard it seemed to her to manage that large school of big boys. Then Joe started to his feet, and said, eagerly,

"But I'll help ye, Miss Mason. I'll do any thing I can to help ye." And then, like a gleam of sunshine amidst April showers, the old roguish twinkle came into his eye, as he added—"I guess the rest of the boys won't trouble you much. They'll do pretty much as I want 'em to!" And so it was. Joe helped Miss Mason, and she had no more trouble in managing the school. She had won Joe's confidence and affection by her kindness, and he became the best boy in the school.

"Blessed are the meek." There are three

ways in which meekness is a blessing. *The first is, by saving us from trouble. The second is, by doing good to ourselves. The third is, by doing good to others.*

And if you wish to be really meek, and have the blessing that Jesus here speaks of, you must become Christians. You must learn to love Jesus, and be like Him. Sometimes we see persons who call themselves Christians, and are members of the Church, who yet allow themselves to get angry, and give way to very bad tempers whenever anything is said to them which they don't like. What shall we say of such persons? There is only one thing to say of them. *They are not Christians!* The Bible says; "If any man have not the spirit of Christ, he is none of His." If we indulge in bad tempers, and allow ourselves to get angry, don't let us say that we don't mean any harm by it; and that isn't very wrong. *It is very wrong.* It is dreadfully wicked. It shows that we are not Christians, and that we are not fit to go to heaven. We should be very sorry for these sinful tempers. We should ask Jesus to forgive us, to take away all angry feelings from us, and make us meek and gentle as He is. Then we shall know what He meant when He said,—"*Blessed are the meek.*"

X.

The Blessedness of Enduring Temptation.

"Blessed is the man that endureth temptation."
JAMES i. 12.

X.

"Blessed is the man that endureth temptation." JAS i. 12.

ONE of the meanings of the word "temptation" is trial. And the word "endure" means to bear. And if we put these two words in the place of those used in the text, then it will read in this way:—"Blessed is the man that beareth trial." We all have a great many trials, or temptations to bear, here in this world. Our life is made up of trials. As soon as we can tell our right hand from the left;—as soon as we know right from wrong, we are put on trial. And we are *kept* on trial, as long as we live in this world. When Adam and Eve were placed in the garden of Eden they were put on trial. There was only one law that they had to keep. That was the law, or command, not to eat of the tree of knowledge. That law was given them to try them. If they had kept it, they would have borne the trial, or endured the temptation appointed for them there, and then they would have been blessed. But they did not bear that trial; they did not keep God's law. They ate of the tree of which God said they should not eat; and then they were thrust out of the garden.

And, in the same way, God's commandments are the things by which we are tried. God commands us to honor and obey our parents. He commands us to keep the Sabbath day holy; not to swear, or steal, or tell lies. And every day of our lives we are put on trial to see if we will keep them.

And so when we read in the Bible that God commands us to repent, and believe in Jesus, and love and serve Him, we are put on trial by these commands. If we do repent and believe, and give our hearts to Jesus, then we bear this trial, and are blessed. If we neglect this, then we do not endure this trial, and we are not blessed

When you go to Sunday School the laws of the School put you on trial. Now suppose that one of those laws is that "no scholar shall talk to another during the lessons." Another is that "no scholar shall go out of school during the exercises without the leave of the Superintendent." And suppose that the scholar sitting next you asks you to get up, and go out with him, without asking leave. Then that is a trial, or temptation to you. If you get up, and go out, you do not endure the temptation, or bear the trial. But if you keep your seat, and refuse to talk with your neighbor, then you do endure the temptation; you bear the trial, and *that* will bring a blessing to you.

When our text says—"Blessed is the man that endureth temptation," it doesn't mean that it is a blessed thing to be tempted to do what is wrong. But, it means that when we are tempted to do what is wrong, it is a blessed thing to resist the temptation, and not give way to it.

Now I wish to show you that there are

three things we can gain by resisting temptation, or bearing trial; and each of these will be a blessing to us. "Blessed is the man that endureth temptation."

The first thing we gain by enduring temptation, or bearing trial, is—STRENGTH.

If you want your body to grow healthy and strong, you must spend a good deal of time out in the open air, walking, or working, or taking exercise there. But if, instead of doing this, you remain shut up in the house all the time, sitting still, or lying down, you may *live*, but you will always be weak, and sickly, and good for nothing.

You know how it would be with two young plants or trees. Suppose that one of these trees is left in charge of a man who doesn't understand the best way of managing young trees. He is afraid of letting it be exposed to the cold, or to the wind. He plants it in a corner of his cellar. There he thinks it will be sheltered from the heat of the sun in summer and from the frosts and storms of winter.

Well, that is true. But what will be the result upon the tree? Perhaps it won't die. It may live. But its leaves will have a pale, sickly, yellow color. It will shoot out long, straggling branches, without any strength or vigor. It will never be good for anything.

But the other tree is treated very differently. It belongs to a person who knows all about trees. It is planted out in a garden, on the side of a hill. The rain comes down on it. The dew falls gently on it. The sun shines brightly on it. The winds sweep by it. The storms rock it and bend it. Yet it grows. It shoots out great branches that are healthy and strong. The more it is rocked and shaken, the deeper it sends its roots into the soil, and the stronger it becomes. The winds and storms that rock that tree are like the temptations or trials that we have to meet. And when the tree stands up against the wind and resists it, it is just like what we are doing when we endure our temptations, or bear our trials manfully. The rocking of the wind is a blessing to the tree, because it helps to make it stronger.

And just in the same way it is a blessing to us when we endure temptation, because it helps to make us strong to do what is good, and to resist what is evil.

Now I want to tell you about two boys. They were treated just as differently as the two trees that I have spoken of. One of these boys was named Charles Brown. His parents were very rich, but not very wise. Charles was their only child. They resolved to take such care of him that, if they could help it, he never should have anything to trouble, or worry him. When he was a baby they never would let the nurse carry him out unless he was covered up, face and all, to keep the cold air from striking him. They fed him with sop and pap till he was quite a good-sized boy, lest anything as hard as bread should hurt his dear little teeth and gums. He never was washed in cold water, because it might make him cry. He was never allowed to play with other boys, because they were so rough that they might hurt him. His parents never let him run, lest he should fall. They never allowed him to go into the street alone, even when he was a big boy, lest he should be knocked down, or run over. They wouldn't let him go to school at all, for fear of anything happening to him. His mother always warmed his bed at night, and had him covered all up in flannel, lest the sheets of the bed should feel cold to him. He always had his breakfast taken to him in bed before he got up in the morning. He wasn't allowed to wash and dress himself till he was eighteen years old, for fear he should put his hands in water that was too cold, or should fatigue himself with too much exertion. Now you can think what a namby-pamby, miserable sort of a fellow Charlie Brown was. He was as pale as a sheet; as thin as a shadow; as weak as an infant; as ignorant as a jackass; and good for just nothing at all. He never bore any trial. He never "endured any temptation." He never was blessed with any strength.

Before he was of age, he took sick and died of mere weakness. It might have been written on his tombstone that he was *killed by kindness.* This was one boy.

The other boy was very different from this. His name was *Abraham Lincoln.* He was born in Kentucky. His parents were poor. While he was quite young they moved to Indiana, and then to Illinois. They couldn't afford to send him to school. He had to work hard, as soon as he was able. He helped his father to build the log house in which they lived. He split the rails to make the fences round his father's farm. He traded on a flat-boat down the Mississippi. This was hard work to do, and in doing it he had to be thrown into company with a good many bad men and boys. He had many trials to bear, and he bore them well. He had many temptations to endure. He was tempted to learn to drink, to swear, to break the Sabbath, and do other wicked things. But he resisted these temptations. He never yielded to them. He was always honest, and truthful, and sober. He tried to make up for the want of schooling by studying all he could. In this way he managed to pick up a good deal of knowledge and learning. He read his Bible. He feared God, and prayed for His help. He became a lawyer. He was an *honest* lawyer. He held on to what he knew to be right. He was sent to the legislature. Thus he grew strong. He was strong in body, and strong in mind, and strong in soul. He was strong to endure temptation, strong to resist evil, and to do right. He was sent to Congress, and at last he was elected President of the United States. During four years of the most dreadful civil war the world has ever known, he filled that important post. The duties of that office were more difficult while Mr. Lincoln was President than ever they had been before. His position was one of the hardest and most trying that anybody in the world ever had to occupy. Yet he never failed, or fainted. He had become so strong by bearing trials, that he was able to stand up, like a giant, under the heaviest burden that ever a man had to carry. He bore the burden well. The ancients used to think that there was a very strong man named Atlas, and that he carried the world on his shoulders. For four years Mr. Lincoln was the Atlas of this country. He carried the government on his shoulders. And the trials he had passed through made him strong to bear that heavy burden. "Blessed is the man that endureth temptation." The first thing we gain by enduring temptation, or bearing trial, is *strength*. And this is a blessing.

The second thing that we gain by enduring temptation, or bearing trial, is—WORTH.

And this is a blessing too. You know very well that a thing which has been tried, or proved, is much more valuable than one that has never been tried. Here, for instance, are two canes. One is a very beautiful looking cane. It has a gold head. It is very smooth, and highly polished. The wood is hard and heavy. It is what is called iron wood. This cane was made from a war club brought to England in the missionary ship "John Williams," from the island of Fatê, in the Pacific Ocean. That war club was sent to me by Captain Morgan, who formerly commanded that ship. The young men of my Bible class had it turned into this beautiful cane for me. I think a great deal of this cane. But I have never tried it. If I should be attacked by a savage dog, and wanted to hit him a heavy blow, I don't know whether the cane would break or not. I should be afraid to trust it.

But here is another cane. This is a very plain looking one. It is made of a sort of cane that grows in the East Indies. It has an ivory handle, and *looks* like a sword cane, but it isn't. I have *tried* this cane, and know I can depend upon it. In traveling through the Isle of Wight, some years ago, I was sitting by the driver, on the top of the stage, with this cane in my hand. It slipped from me, and fell down between the spokes of the wheel and the body of the stage. This made it bend right short off, just as your arm bends at the elbow. I saw it fall to the ground, and lie there, bent almost at a right angle. I said to myself, "My poor cane is ruined." I asked the driver to stop while I got down to pick up my cane. I picked it up. I bent it across my knee. It straightened right out at once. It wasn't broken. Not a fibre of the wood was started. It was as good as ever. Nay, it was a great deal better than ever. It had been tried, and proved to be a tough, strong cane. That trial had made it more valuable. It had given it worth. And now if I had to choose between these two canes, in preparing to defend myself against a fierce dog, I should take the plain one. If I wanted to make a show, and look fine, of course I should take this handsome, gold-headed cane. But, if I wanted something that I could depend upon in time of danger, I should take the one that had been tried.

When they were recruiting soldiers during the late war, they alwrys offered a great deal more money to one who had already been a year or two in the service, because he had got used to it. He had been *tried*; and the trial through which he had passed made him more valuable than a raw recruit. It gave him worth.

Perhaps nothing will illustrate the benefit or blessedness of bearing trial, better than the change of value that takes place in a piece of iron when it is made into steel. Suppose we have here say an ounce of common iron. This would be worth not more than a penny. Well, suppose now that our ounce of iron has been changed into an ounce of the finest steel. This would be done, according to the old way of making steel, by putting it in a very hot fire, and then pounding it with heavy hammers. And to the iron this would be just the same thing that bearing trials is to us. The Bible compares trial to a furnace, in which we are put, or to a rod or hammer, with which we are beaten. It is a blessing to the iron to be put into the fire, and beaten with the hammer, because that turns it into steel, and so increases its value.

And it is a blessing to us when we bear trials well, because it helps to make us better people. It increases our worth. When an ounce of iron is turned into fine steel it is worth more than gold. An ounce of fine gold is worth about twenty-four dollars. An ounce of the finest steel can be made into the fine hair-like springs that are used in watches. One ounce of steel would make more than three thousand of those springs, and these would sell for about two dollars and a half each. This would make that ounce of steel worth seven thousand five hundred dollars. And so it was a blessed thing for that piece of iron that it was put in the fire and pounded with the hammer, for that increased its value *seven hundred and fifty thousand times.*

There was an old man who lived in a little country village. Everybody called him "Old Willie." He didn't swear, or get drunk. He was not an angry nor dishonest man. The great temptation he had and which he never resisted, was to be *lazy*. He loved every thing better than work. He was not very poor, for he had a nice cottage, with a garden and cornfield, and a meadow for the cow. But he never could be persuaded really to work at anything. He would spend half a day in mending a child's plaything, or getting a boy's skates ready; and he would sit the whole day on a bench before the village shop, nodding or smoking, or talking with anybody who was willing to spend an idle hour.

The great complaint of "Old Willie" was that he "never had any luck in anything." His hard-working neighbors were always "lucky," but *he* never was. Everything went against him. If he planted a strip of corn, the fences not being in good condition, some strolling cow would get in, and in one night spoil it all. Then he would say he was "unlucky" with his corn. If he had a cow of his own, she was sure to dry up very soon, for want of proper food and care, and then he "was unlucky with his cow." If he got a pig, it would squeal all day for something to eat; and at night it would get out and run away. He would have great trouble in hunting it up, and then he "was unlucky with his pig." If there came a rain storm, he was so unlucky as to have a house that was always leaking for want of a little work upon it. His kind, patient wife had caught a bad cold in the leaky house, and was laid up a great part of the time with rheumatism, and he was very unlucky in this. And often when he had spent the week in idleness, he would spend the Sunday in fishing, in the great pond near the village, so as to get something for his family to eat.

But there was one treasure "Old Willie" had which he loved better than any thing else in the world. This was a beautiful little daughter, about ten years old. One summer a Sunday School was started some distance from the village. Mary wanted very much to go to it. Her father wouldn't let her go alone, so he used to take her to the school. When he left her at the door he would lounge about the neighborhood smoking, till the school was out, and then he would take Mary home again. One day he went and stood under the window to listen to the children singing.

The Superintendent saw him, and kindly invited him in. He went in, and after that he would often take a seat near the door and listen to what was said. This set him to thinking, and sometimes great tears would roll down his cheeks. Little Mary had learned to love Jesus, and to pray to Him.

One night "Old Willie" heard her praying for her "dear father." This was too much for him. He began to think it was time for him to pray for himself. He did so. He soon became a Christian, and then, O, what a change took place! He resolved to give way to laziness no longer. He resisted this temptation. He turned over a new leaf. He became an industrious, hard-working man. And then how soon everything about him improved! What he used to call his "bad luck," all disappeared. He left off wasting his time on the bench before the village shop, and spent it in working. He stopped fishing on Sunday. His house was mended; his corn grew and flourished; his cow became a different creature; his pig stopped squealing, and his wife got better. "Old things passed away, and all things became new" with him. He learned to resist the great temptation which had overcome him, and he found himself blessed in doing it. He became a better man—ten times more valuable than he had been before. The second thing we gain by enduring temptation is *worth*.

The third thing we gain by it is HONOR.

God has put some things together in such a way that we never can separate them. If you go and stand in the sun, will your body cast a shadow on the ground? Yes. Can you possibly stand in the sun without casting a shadow somewhere? No. If you fire off a gun, will it make a noise? Yes. Can you fire off a gun without its making a noise? No. If you put your finger in the fire, will it hurt you? Yes. Can you put your finger in the fire without its hurting you? No. And the reason is, that God has bound these things together so that nobody can separate them. And just in the same way God has connected honor with resisting temptation; and shame or dishonor with not resisting it. And nobody can separate these things.

I wish to give you some illustrations to show you that this is always so. If we endure or resist temptation, we shall be blessed by bringing honor on ourselves. If we give way to temptation we shall be punished by bringing shame or dishonor on ourselves. I have one illustration about two angels, one about two men, and one about a boy.

The first illustration is about two angels. More than six thousand years ago, before our world was made, there were two angels in heaven. The name of one was Lucifer, the name of the other was Gabriel. God made them both holy and good. But they were both tempted to rebel against the government of God. Lucifer did not resist the temptation. He yielded to it. He got a good many other angels to unite with him. They wanted to set up a government of their own, independent of God. They were all driven out of heaven, and thrust down to hell. There, Lucifer, who is the Devil, or Satan, has been their leader ever since in all kinds of wickedness. He has never had a moment of peace or happiness ever since then. He is the tempter of men. He is a liar, and a murderer. He is "the wicked one." Every body despises him. All evil is traced up to him. The deepest shame—the darkest dishonor, are his now, and will be heaped on his head forever. He will be shut up in the bottomless pit, with swearers, and liars, and thieves, and murderers, and all the worst sort of people forever. He did not resist temptation, and this shame and dishonor are the result of it.

But look at Gabriel on the other hand. He endured, or resisted temptation. He would not join in the rebellion against God. And what was the consequence? He remained in heaven. He "kept his first estate." He continued holy, and good, and happy. He "stands in the presence of God." He is engaged in doing good. We read in the Bible how God sent him once with a message to Daniel the prophet. Dan. ix. 21, 22. About five hundred years after, he was sent again to tell of the birth of John the Baptist, and of our Saviour. Luke i. 19, 26. And he is, no doubt, employed in the same way still. To stand in God's presence, and serve him, is the highest honor that an angel can have in heaven. Gabriel has this honor. And thus he was blessed for enduring temptation. He gained honor by it. This is the illustration about two angels.

We next take an illustration from two men. These men were both connected with the American Revolution. The name of one of them was Benedict Arnold. He was a general in the American army at that time. He was a very brave soldier, but not a good man. He was put on trial for bad conduct. It was proved that he had acted in a way that was very wrong for an officer in the army. And it was ordered by Congress that he should be reproved for his conduct by the commander-in-chief. General Washington made the reproof as gentle as possible, on account of his having been such a good soldier. But Arnold could not bear this. It made him very angry. Instead of confessing his faults, and trying to do better, he made up his mind to revenge himself at once on Washington, on Congress, and on his country.

Through the kindness of General Washington, he was appointed to the command of West Point, on the North River. This was one of the strongest and most important fortresses held by the American army. Arnold knew that the loss of that fortress would be one of the heaviest blows that could fall on his struggling country. Yet he *basely resolved to betray West Point into the hands of the enemy.* He wrote to Sir Henry Clinton, the commander of the British army, to know what they would give him if he should deliver up that place to them, with all the soldiers, the arms, and ammunition that were in it.

Of course the English general was glad enough to get such an offer. It was agreed between them that Arnold should have the same rank in the English army that he held in the American. And besides that, he was to get thirty thousand pounds sterling, or about a hundred and fifty thousand dollars, to reward him for his treachery. But just when he was on the point of finishing the bargain, and of delivering that important post over to the British, the plot was found out. He was obliged to flee for his life. He managed to escape, and get over to the English army. But though he saved his life, he lost the reward he expected to get. And what was more than that, he lost his character. Every honorable officer and soldier in the English army despised him. Like Judas Iscariot, who betrayed his Master, Benedict Arnold betrayed his country. He became *a traitor!* *That* is one of the most shameful things that can be said of a man. Arnold's name is covered with the blackest disgrace. As long as the world stands, that disgrace will last. Trial was laid upon him, but he could not bear it. The result has been shame and dishonor.

The other person I refer to, and whom I would put by the side of Arnold, as showing the honor that results from bearing trial, or enduring temptation, is *George Washington.* He was as brave a soldier as Arnold, and a much better man. God raised him up to be the father of his people—the saviour of his country. He had many trials to bear—much heavier than those that were laid on Arnold, but Washington bore his trials nobly. The people often found fault with him for what he did; but he never got angry, or thought for a moment of revenging himself on them, as Arnold had done. Some of his own officers formed a wicked plot against him, to have him put out of his high office. He found out that plot. But it had no other effect on him than to make him try to do his duty, and to serve his country better than ever. He endured every temptation, he bore every trial well. And what is the result? The name of *Washington* has been covered with glory to the ends of the world. He has gained the greatest honor by enduring temptation. Benedict Arnold the traitor — and George Washington the patriot — what a contrast between them! In that contrast how clearly we see the blessedness of enduring temptation!

But now for the illustration about the boy. It is a story that may be called "The Gold Medal; or, The Brave Boy Rewarded." It's a little long, but it's so good that I think you won't mind that.

There was an academy in a country village in England. Among the scholars was one named James Hartley, and another, Edward Jemson. Hartley was a new scholar. His parents were honest, respectable people, but not very rich. He was a bright, manly boy. Most of the other boys were the sons of wealthy parents. One morning, as a company of them were going to school, they saw Hartley coming along the lane, driving a cow to a field a little beyond the school. "Halloo! Hartley," said Jemson—" what's the price of milk?" " What do you fodder on, Jim?" asked another. " Well done, boys," said a third. " If you want to see the latest Paris style, look at those boots!"

Hartley waved his hand and smiled pleasantly as he passed, without saying a word. He drove the cow to the field, took down the bars, put her safely in, put up the bars, and then went into school with the rest. At the close of the afternoon, he let the cow out, and drove her off, none of the boys knew where. He did this every day for two or three weeks. It caused a great wondering among the boys. They knew that Hartley's father didn't keep a cow, and as James didn't choose to explain why he did this, they couldn't tell what to make of it. Most of the boys were of that foolish class who look upon any honest labor as a sort of disgrace. And so they made all sorts of fun about Hartley and his cow.

" Well, Jim, how's the 'ke-ow' to-day?" was a question often asked him.

"I suppose, Hartley," said Jemson to him one day, "I suppose your daddy means to make a milkman of you?"

"Why not?" asked Hartley.

"Oh, nothing; only don't leave too much water in the cans when you rinse them—that's all," said he.

Then the boys had a hearty laugh. Hartley never got angry. He bore it all with the greatest good humor, and only said—"Never fear, boys; if I ever should rise to be a milkman, you may be sure of one thing—I'll give good measure, and good milk."

The day after this conversation there was a public examination in the Academy. A number of ladies and gentlemen from the neighboring towns were present. After the examination, prizes were given to the best scholars, and Hartley and Jemson, who were the smartest boys in the school, both received prizes. After these had been distributed, the principal of the school said there was one prize consisting of a gold medal, which was not often given, because it was seldom that any one was entitled to it. It was the prize not of scholarship, but of HEROISM. The last boy who received it was young Manners, who, three years ago, saved a blind girl from drowning at the risk of his own life. And now, with the permission of the company, I wish to relate a short story.

Not long since, some of the scholars belonging to this academy were flying a kite in an adjoining lane, just as a poor boy on horseback rode by, on his way to the mill. The horse took fright and threw the boy off, injuring the boy so badly that he was carried home, and confined to his bed for some weeks. None of the boys who had occasioned this misfortune went to inquire about the wounded boy. One scholar, however, not among the kite flyers, saw the accident. He went to inquire after the boy who was hurt, and ask if he could be of any help. .

He soon found that the wounded boy was the grandson of a poor widow, whose only support consisted in selling the milk of a very fine cow, of which she was the owner.

When she saw her poor boy brought in wounded, she said—"Oh, dear, what shall we do? for I am old and lame, and now there is no one to take care of the cow."

"Never mind, good woman," said the scholar, "I'll drive your cow till your boy gets well again."

"God bless you, my good fellow," said the old woman, while she wept the thanks she could not speak. But the scholar's kindness did not stop here. He found that money was wanted to buy medicine.

"I have money that my mother gave me to buy a pair of boots with," said he, "but I can do without them for awhile."

"Oh, no," said the old woman, "I can't consent to that: but here is a pair of heavy boots that I bought for Henry. He can't wear them now, and if you would only buy them, giving what they cost, we could get on nicely."

The scholar bought the boots, clumsy as they were, and has worn them up to this time.

Well, when it was discovered by the other boys of the academy that our scholar was in the habit of driving a cow, they heaped all sorts of ridicule upon him. They especially made fun of his clumsy, cow-hide boots. But he kept cheerfully on, day after day, not foolishly trying to keep out of sight, but bravely doing his duty. The laughs, and jokes, and sneers of his companions were a temptation to him to give up. But he resisted this temptation. He persevered in driving the cow, and wearing the thick boots, because he felt he was doing right. He wouldn't tell the boys why he was doing this, because that would look like praising himself. And he didn't mind the fun they made of him, because he knew it was a feeling of false pride which led them to think that it was a disgrace to be engaged in any honest employment. I only found it out by accident yesterday.

"And now, ladies and gentlemen," said the teacher, "I appeal to you, if there was not *true heroism* in this boy's conduct? Nay, Master Hartley, don't creep out of sight behind the black-board! You were not afraid of ridicule, you mustn't be afraid of praise. Come out, Master James Hartley, and let us see your honest face!"

Hartley came out blushing like a rose, and the whole company broke out into loud applause of his noble conduct. The ladies stood upon the benches and waved their handkerchiefs. The old men wiped the tears from their eyes, while the young men clapped their hands, and gave three cheers for the brave boy. Even the clumsy boots on Hartley's feet seemed like a brighter ornament than a crown could have been on his head. And then the teacher put the gold medal round Hartley's neck, to honor him for resisting temptation, and doing right. He was blessed in the honor that he gained.

"Blessed is the man that endureth temptation." We have spoken of three things gained by enduring temptation, and which make up this blessing. What is the first? *Strength.* What is the second? *Worth.* And what is the third? *Honor.*

Now, my dear young friends, don't forget that you have to meet trials and temptations every day you live, and in every place that you go to. You can't get away from them while you are in this world. If you only learn to resist them and get into the habit of doing this, then you will be blessing yourselves all the time. Every day you will be growing in *strength*, in *worth*, in *honor*. But you can't do this of yourself. You must pray for Jesus to help you. And if you only get His help, you will be sure to succeed. He endured temptation Himself when He was on earth, and He knows how to help us. Pray earnestly and constantly to Him, and then you will be sure to get the blessing promised to those who endure temptations.

THE END.

INDEX.

www.ingramcontent.com/pod-product-compliance
Lightning Source LLC
LaVergne TN
LVHW020214110826
845151LV00003B/709

* 9 7 8 1 4 2 5 5 3 3 8 4 7 *